90 Seconds to Yes

Patrice Bonnell & Shelly Goff

With Honorary Forward by

Dr. Jeannie Ju, DDS

ISBN:
978-1-64059-002-1

Forward

When Patrice and Shelly asked me to write a forward for their book, I was absolutely honored, excited and at the same time scared. Why scared? Scared to admit that I was a dentist who has zero percent knowledge of how to run a dental practice. I know this as a fact because when I bought an existing practice, it kicked my butt hard. It was so hard it hurt me mentally, physical and emotionally and I felt like a failure to my husband, my son, my parents and myself.

And, then I met Patrice and Shelly. Here's what I think of them:

PATRICE AND SHELLY = AWESOME.

Let me say that again.

PATRICE AND SHELLY = AWESOME.

Meeting these two amazing women has been the best thing to ever happen to me. And, then you might ask, "What about saying my son and my husband are the best things to ever happen to me?" Don't successful people in the movies say that? The reason why I say Patrice and Shelly is because without them, I would not be able to give all my heart and soul to my beautiful son and loving husband, while also living out my dream as a successful private practice dentist. And, if you ask my staff, a very cool boss, too.

Let me tell you a little bit about my life as a dentist and how that all changed for the better when I met Patrice and Shelly. I really thought the minute I got my dental degree, life was going to be super good. I would drive a nice car, wear nice clothes, make money while helping others, patients would love me and the staff would think I was the best boss ever. Could I ever be so wrong? Yes, I was absolutely wrong. Not 99% wrong, but 100% wrong.

I realize I was wrong just a few hours into my first job at a corporate dental group as an associate dentist. I jumped from associate job to another associate job for the next 3 years before I realized they were all the same, just with a different company name. So, then I decided to be my own boss and purchased a private dental practice just a week before I gave birth to my son. (I would never do that again. Let me clarify - you can buy a private practice and have a kid but just don't do it at the same time. Being sleep deprived and taking over a dental practice isn't easy unless you have super human powers. Seriously, there's a reason why you need maternity leave.) I thought the minute I signed that purchase contract, life was surely going to be good. Because, isn't that how it goes?

Here's a short version of my miserable first two years of ownership:

- The existing staff all quit on me by the end of 2 years.
- We were struggling to keep our schedule full.
- Patients needed treatment but no one was scheduling.
- Money was so low in our bank account I wasn't sure if we could make payroll, not once but several times.
- Personal and business credit card debt was increasing.
- Patients didn't trust me and if I wasn't careful with what I said, they would chew me out.
- I had no idea how to deal with patients' complaints and objections.
- I had no idea how to deal with my staff's complaints and objections.
- I was clueless about dental insurance and didn't realize I was losing money by accepting certain plans.
- The existing practice was a $1 million dollar practice and then with me as the owner, it became an $800k practice.

- Many, many sleepless nights.
- A lot of stress.
- Crying in the closet.

Patrice and Shelly changed all that 360 degrees. I have never been happier in my life and feel that I finally am now able to say I am living the good life. If you can see the way my face lightens up when I mention their names, then you will know how happy they have made my life. I learned from them how to increase my revenue, drop HMO plans, work less days, see less patients per day, increase case acceptance, create a fun and positive work culture, find patients who appreciate my work and coach my staff to be my dream team. They have trained to me be a great leader for my team, a great dentist for my patients, and a great business owner. I can't imagine my life without them. With their help, I bought another dental practice and now we are a $2 million dollar practice!

Patrice and Shelly are the best of the best in the business. They customize their management strategies to you and it's not cookie cutter. Okay, so I have only worked with them for about 2 years and I have not worked with all the other dental consultants out there in this field to compare, but to me they are the absolute best. If you don't trust me from reading this, please look me up and call me so I can convince you otherwise.

I think it's so awesome that they are sharing their knowledge with you in this book. I am excited for you as you begin your journey with Patrice and Shelly. And, as an added bonus, if you hang out with them long enough, they'll share their Snapchats with you.

Patrice and Shelly, thank you for everything and thank you for helping others just like me.

Jeannie Ju, DDS, Owner
Creative Smiles – Tucson AZ

CONTENTS

Introduction

Every day, you and more than two million other dentists worldwide don your white coats and go off to work, focused on two primary goals:

1. to practice dentistry to the highest standards you can
2. to build a thriving, personally fulfilling and financially rewarding practice

All your years at university and dental school prepared you with a solid foundation to help you achieve that first goal. But how much time and attention did your years of study give you toward the second?

If you've received any business-building advice at all, you might have received a cursory overview of management, accounting, or basic marketing – if you're lucky. As a matter of fact, a study published by the ***Journal of Dental Education*** reported that while two thirds of the dental schools in the United States encouraged coursework in business, **none of them required it.**

Think about it. In an average workday, you might deal with a severely apprehensive patient, a performance issue with someone on your team, a vendor or suppler who isn't delivering, accounts receivable or insurance reimbursement problems, or complicated government regulations. Did your years of university education prepare you for all of that?

Now add the pressure of generating enough revenue to repay what might be staggering student loans, increasing overhead, and high premiums for dental practice insurance, with enough left over to assure you and your family a comfortable, secure livelihood.

If you're a dentist in private practice, you're like one of the thousands of satellites in orbit – doing your job, flying solo, and trying your best not to crash and burn. It's no wonder that the stress and anxiety of today's dental business environment can increase to the point where some flee the profession altogether.

A slow-and-steady, learn-as-you-go, one-foot-in-front-of-the-other approach to building and managing your practice is just not going to cut it.

There's a better way. That's why we wrote this book.

An old adage says, *"If you keep doing what you've always done, you'll keep getting what you've always got."* If you can open yourself to the possibility that what you're doing isn't working to the level you desire and that you do not have all the answers you need, you can objectively examine your own leadership, management, and relationship skills and discover how to genuinely serve your patients and your team.

This book is for you if you want to:

- Create a 5-star experience for your patients so you can grow your new patient base and make them loyal patients for life
- Encourage your patients to willingly accept your treatment plans – in 90 seconds or less
- Increase your practice revenue by 20% each year
- Build a dedicated, high-performing team who's excited to work with you
- Achieve more by working less
- Create the thriving, personally fulfilling, financially rewarding practice you deserve.

Ready? Let's get started.

CHAPTER 1

It's Monday morning after a long weekend. You're wondering what chaos will greet you when you walk into the office.

After a shower, a bite of breakfast, and goodbye kisses with the family, you head out the back door. As you reach for the car keys, you think to yourself, "When I make more money, I'm going to get that new car."

As you slowly back out of the driveway and make your way down the same familiar street in the same familiar car, you can't help but wonder whether you closed the garage door. You're already distracted, considering everything you have to do today.

"Oh, how I wish I had more time in my day to get everything done!"

Traffic isn't bad, and glancing at your watch, you realize you have enough time to swing by Starbucks for a caffeine jolt to set you up for the day ahead. As you turn into the drive-through lane, you debate whether you should return the stack of patient calls from the weekend that have been hanging over you like a dark cloud, call back the sales rep who will not leave you alone since you visited his website last month

(6 emails, 3 texts and 1 voicemail!)

or just take a minute for yourself and listen to the music YOU want to listen to since your kids aren't in the car. You finally settle for the music. It helps you tune everything out for just a few minutes as you slowly inch your way toward the pickup window.

You sit behind the wheel, watching the kids in the car in front of you laugh with their friends and happily sing as loud as they can to the new song on the radio. It reminds you of days past, when life was easier and more carefree -- when your biggest worry was deciding where to hang out with your friends. Ah, the good old days!

Finally, the girl in the drive-thru window is handing you your drink with a big smile. She makes eye contact, and genuinely asks how your day is going, waiting for you to answer. She takes a moment to make sure you got everything you asked for. Then she personally recommends a new breakfast roll that she swears would taste incredible with your drink. You're not hungry but you just can't say no to her infectious sincerity.

As you pay for your drink and breakfast roll, you think to yourself, "Wow, I wish this girl would come work for me. The patients would love her and we probably wouldn't have to put up with all the drama we have now...and she just sold me a sugar roll that I really didn't want or need! How did that happen? Anyhow, Megan could train her and she could become my new treatment coordinator and that would mean more patients would accept treatment and I could take my family on that beach trip they have been begging for. This could actually work!"

As you drive around the narrow drive-through back out onto the street, that fleeting fantasy escapes you. You're back to that familiar debate: listen to music to pump you up for the day or begrudgingly make the calls you know you need to make. Ugh, there is no choice, only salvation. Music.

You pull into your parking space at the office. You have ten minutes before your first scheduled patient of the morning shows up.

You morning huddle was supposed to start five minutes ago, and your assistant is running late again for whatever the reason is this time. A bit disgruntled, you start your huddle without her...only to have your first patient show up early. You quickly sprint through the rundown of what is important in today's schedule, ask if we're meeting goal, and then you realize:

No one really has it together. This is just organized chaos.

Your hygienist announces she is going on vacation with her family for two weeks next month (must be nice). Your receptionist reminds you her review and raise are two months past due. As she walks away, your office manager hands you a note from UPS letting you know they could not deliver your order because the office was closed. Hygiene's first patient is a no-show even though he was confirmed yesterday. So you ask your hygienist to make recare calls, but she tells you she would prefer to sharpen instruments instead. After all, calling patients is the front office's job, not hers.

Breathe. Just breathe...

The receptionist seats your patient (a crown seat) because your assistant still has not shown up. No one seems to know where the patient's lab case is. Dread is washing over you, as your day is already spiraling out of control. You glance at the computer to check the time, and you're shocked. It's only 8:05am.

There ***must*** *be a better way...*

Sadly, for far too many, this is reality.

Yours is a high-stress, high-risk profession, where anxiety affects patients and their dentist alike. Anxiety and stress not only wreak havoc on your personal health and well-being, they wreak havoc on your team, your family, and your practice as well.

You probably chose this profession out of a genuine desire to help and serve people, never really anticipating the degree of physical and mental work the profession requires.

Think about it.

You are now responsible for budgets, bills, collections, recruiting, hiring, training, supervising, marketing, equipment maintenance, purchasing, management, paperwork, insurance, regulatory compliance, P&L, ROI, and everything else that accompanies being a business owner...while at the same time presenting a cool, efficient, caring professional demeanor with patients who are sometimes nervous, frightened, forgetful, or downright flaky.

It's no wonder so many dentists burn out and quit the profession within 10 years – great, talented dentists simply walk away from their careers due to the constant, never-ending overload and resulting stress.

All they ever wanted was to perform excellent dentistry, in a successful practice that runs like a well-oiled machine.

So is it reasonable for you to expect to have to work this hard for the rest of your life?

Absolutely Not!

That is why we wrote this book. We promise you there is absolutely a better, easier way!

This book will give you simple strategies to lead your team to true excellence and deliver that 5 – Star experience so your patients say "Yes" in 90 seconds or less so you can go back to doing what you love easily and effortlessly.

In this book, you will discover simple strategies to help you transform your practice, create a super-star team of dedicated, self-managing professionals, and a roster of loyal, satisfied patients who provide you a steady stream of referrals.

Here's what you'll learn:

- Begin at the beginning: how to create a mindset that sets you up for success
- How to avoid "information overload" and the havoc it creates
- How to set up streamlined, efficient systems and get your team to follow them so your practice will practically run itself
- How to create a superstar team of CEOs
- How to create consistent, effective hand offs
- How to establish rapport with even the most difficult people
- Why focusing on "them" is more powerful than focusing on "you"
- How to establish a treatment plan so effective your patients will say "yes" in 90 seconds or less —while they thank you for the "5-Star Service"
- What to do next: refining your skills for even more success

If you're ready to transform your practice, and in the process, transform not only your life but also the lives of your team and your patients, let's start by exploring the mindset that success and leadership requires.

CHAPTER 2

Begin at the Beginning: Understand Your Role as a Dentist and Business Owner

Have you ever wondered what makes one dental practice different from another? Why is one practice thriving while another, in the same neighborhood, struggles to survive?

The difference is Leadership and Business Management Skills.

When we first started working with dentists on the business aspects of their practices, we discovered many doctors -- with remarkable clinical skills -- struggling just to make their practices profitable.

Of course you must have strong clinical skills or you'll never attract or retain patients. But you must realize the best margins or the most expensive, top-of-the-line cosmetic cases will not make your practice successful all by themselves.

Attend an ADA – or any other prominent meeting for that matter – and you'll notice that seminars on the latest crown or implant technique fill up first, while the sessions about practice management are always very sparsely attended.

Why do you think that is?

We simply shift toward what is familiar and avoid (or fear) what is unknown or unfamiliar. After all, you probably didn't invest all that time and money on your education because you wanted to be a businessperson. Performing high-quality dentistry is familiar. You were trained for it. Running a business? That's a whole different matter, requiring a different set of skills.

If you're one of the many dentists who want someone else to manage the day-to-day business of your practice (office manager, spouse, front office) so you can focus on what you do best, you might be unconsciously setting up your practice for failure, simply by avoiding the unfamiliar.

The truth is that you, the owner— the dentist— are the person with the greatest financial risk. **You are the person with the responsibility to create a**

thriving, growing, healthy practice. You simply cannot delegate that responsibility. It just doesn't make sense.

You want to understand the fundamentals of management. You want to have solid business systems in place to take care of your patients; from the moment they call your office to the moment they complete their treatment. You want to lead and direct your team to help your practice not only survive, but to thrive and grow.

What makes a dental practice successful?

In over 20 years of working with dentists, we have found that the most successful dental practices not only strive to master clinical skills, they expand their focus to include four key areas:

- Implement well-designed, effective business systems
- Recruit, hire, and train high-performing team members
- Learn from professionals how to be influential with yourself, your team, your patients and everyone you encounter
- Lead and inspire your team to succeed

The practices that focus on these four key areas perform head and shoulders above their competition, and experience faster and more predictable growth. Their practices don't just survive...they prosper.

When we first meet with new clients, we find many doctors want financial success **now** however are "stuck" with which direction to go (Hire new staff, train existing staff, new patient marketing, purchasing the newest technology, etc.).

Once we get our client's focused on what will truly make their practice successful, **many have experienced up to a 40% revenue increase -- within the first 90 days.**

If you want to see the same transformative results in your practice, you need to expand your vision of yourself beyond just being the dentist – you want to envision yourself as a leader. **See yourself as the CEO of your practice, your business and your economy.**

Once you accept responsibility for leading your team, being the CEO "at cause" in the success or failure of your practice, your team can unite to support you and help you reach your goals. As your practice starts thriving, the experience can be transformative: not only for you, but also for your team, your patients, and your profitability.

In other words, **you want to be "at cause" for what you want.**

But before you can be at cause for what you want, you have to define exactly what that is. Consider and reflect on how you see your own role in your practice, and examine whether what you have been doing has produced the kinds of results you want, the kind you deserve.

Questions for reflection:

1. Why did you choose to become a dentist? What is it about the profession that is most fulfilling or rewarding to you?

2. What are your strengths and limitations as a "businessperson?" What are you best at? Where could you use some help? What are you avoiding?

3. Did your education provide any business management, leadership, or communication skills training? If so, how many hours? What classes did you take? What have you applied?

4. What specific results would you like your practice to generate in terms of income, patient load, staff levels, and personal and professional satisfaction? What would "taking your practice to the next level" look like?

5. What have you done, or are you currently doing, to take your practice to the next level? Is it working?

In the next chapter, we will start to explore the tools that will help you develop the kind of leadership mindset that will help you create exactly the practice you want.

Contact us at www.dmicoaching.com for assistance

Chapter 3

Your Mindset

Set Yourself and Your Practice Up for Success with a Powerful Leadership Mindset

"Whether you think you can, or you think you can't – you're right." ~ Henry Ford

Everyone has the ability to lead; we just need to learn how to use the tools that awaken the leader inside us. The first, most important of these tools is "mindset," a system of beliefs and thoughts that support us as leaders.

If you've been reluctant to step into your role as a leader, happier being just the "dentist in the dental practice" who is content to let somebody else manage your business; or if you've been avoiding taking on the responsibilities associated with being a businessperson (budgeting, accounting, management, hiring, training, marketing or any other aspect of business), there is an underlying mindset at work. That mindset consists of beliefs operating in the background that can prevent us from stepping out and moving forward.

Beliefs like, *"I'm not good at marketing or self-promotion," "I not a salesman," "I shouldn't have to do all the work myself," "I'm too old to learn how to market myself on social media," "There isn't enough time to get everything done,"* or any other thought pattern like these, keep us stuck right where we are.

In other words, if you believe you can't, you're right. And you probably won't.

Millions of words have been written on the power of positive thinking and the link between our thoughts about reality and reality itself, and you've probably read a few hundred thousand of them. Some of the great purveyors of these ideas include Anthony Robbins, Brian Tracy, Norman Vincent Peale, Earl Nightingale, Stephen Covey, and countless others. If you haven't read any of these "thought masters," you owe it to yourself to explore them.

You'll find that all of these great thinkers share one basic philosophy: your experience of life is quite literally generated by the thoughts running through your mind and the beliefs that support them. If you accept that as true, then it only makes sense that if you want to create a different experience of reality, you must start by creating a different pattern of thoughts and beliefs.

To step into your role as business owner, leader, and CEO of your practice, you'll need to develop a pattern of thoughts and beliefs that support you in that role. In our work with successful dental practices, we've uncovered four basic beliefs that are the foundation of the Success Mindset that supports the leaders of those practices.

4 Beliefs Essential for Leadership Success

1. **There is no failure, only feedback**

   "I didn't fail: I successfully found 10,000 ways that didn't work." ~ Thomas Edison

   If Thomas Edison had given up after his first attempt at creating the incandescent lightbulb, we might very well still be sitting in the dark. Whenever you set out to do something new, it might take you a while to get it right. Great things often do. But if you give up and quit because you tried a few times without success, and then consider the entire effort a failure, then you really have failed.

Business, finance, and motivation author Robert Allen once said, "there is no such thing as failure, only feedback." So you try something. You fail. The way to respond is to say to yourself, "Well, that didn't work!" and look for the lesson. The lesson revealed in every failed attempt to try something new, once you learn it, is one less thing standing in your way.

To see how true this belief is, just reflect back on your time in school. Were you able to create a perfect filling your first time behind the mask?

Adopting this core belief will help you because it works in concert with the next belief.

2. The more flexible I can be, the greater my chances of success

"The definition of insanity is doing the same thing over and over again and expecting a different result." ~ Albert Einstein

In plain, simple English, it's clear that if what you are doing is not getting the result you want, then you should do something different. That requires your willingness to admit that what you're doing isn't working and it's time to explore different solutions. That's flexibility.

The more flexible you can be, and the more willing you are to adapt your approach, the more likely you are to discover an approach that works best. Using Thomas Edison as an example, whenever an experiment did not work, he altered the next experiment in some way. This example clearly demonstrates that we learn more from our failures than we do from our successes, thus creating feedback that tells us to try again in a new and different way.

For example, if your treatment acceptance rate is only at 30%, re-evaluate your approach, your team's approach, your timing, the language you use, your listening skills, and any other aspect of proposing your treatment plan. Be prepared to adapt your approach for greater success.

3. Respect people's individuality

"Seek first to understand, then to be understood." ~ Stephen Covey

Every human being on Earth is gifted with a unique personality, composed of a unique set of wants, needs, hopes, fears, likes, dislikes, goals, ambitions, desires, wishes, beliefs, and opinions. And thank goodness for that. It's what makes being in the "people business" so fascinating.

The more willing you are to let people be exactly the way they are, and exactly the way they are not, the more likely you will be able to influence them.

If you take the time to discover and discuss with your patients what *they* are thinking and feeling, what *they* value, what is important to *them*, they may trust you and become more open to your influence. Remember, you are not in the tooth business; you are in the People Business.

4. If I can't do something at present, I can learn to do it

"Education is what remains after one has forgotten what one has learned in school."
Albert Einstein

Albert Einstein was a poor student. Frustrated by an educational system that favored learning by rote repetition, his greatest breakthroughs arose out of his commitment to learning and thinking his own way, and that commitment spanned the course of his life.

Successful dentists realize that they, too, can learn to improve themselves and their relationships with their teams and their patients, if they are committed to learning what they don't presently know. Each of us learns differently, and for each of us the keys to successful learning will be as unique as we are. Using the right tools, asking effective questions, dedicating time to practice, and breaking down new tasks into bite-size chunks can help you learn a new insights.

Perhaps the fastest way to learn a new skill is to ask for help when you need it, from someone who is skilled at the task you want to learn, such as a consultant, coach, or mentor. Let your curiosity guide you in learning new skills. Learn from their successes, their failures, and their insights.

Ideas for Action: How to Make this Mindset Your Own

Embodying these four beliefs and making them an integral part of your own mindset will not happen all by itself. You need to add three actions to cement these beliefs in place:

1. **Realize challenges are simply opportunities**: Relish challenges as opportunities for growth, development and improvement. Put fear aside to try something new and keep at it until you achieve excellence.

2. **Replace "failing" with "learning":** Oprah Winfrey was fired from her job as a evening news reporter in Baltimore because her producer felt she was "too emotionally invested in her stories" and she was "unfit for television". Bill Belichick was fired from his first head coaching job with the Cleveland Browns. Walt Disney was fired from the Kansas City Star because he "lacked imagination". Stephen King's most renowned book "Carrie" was rejected 30 times before it was finally accepted. Imagine if these icons were stuck in the mindset of "failure" and gave in to the rejection. Our world would be very different! Failure is quite simply an external event that gives us an opportunity to take risks and learn. Actively search for flaws in your systems and services and refine them for excellence.

3. **Take Action:** The most successful people are those who tried many approaches until they found the one that worked. Instead of talking about what they were going to do, they just did it. Go from inspiration to action and find and the resources necessary to make the changes you desire. Be at Cause for yourself, your business and your life!

Now that we've explored the four beliefs critical to a successful mindset, we'll show you how to use this mindset to develop a patient-centric practice – a practice that delivers "5-Star Service" and delights your patients so that they become a non-stop source of glowing testimonials and referrals to your business.

Chapter 4

Turn Your Loyal Patients into Raving Fans by Providing 5-Star Service

A general dentist in a mid-sized Colorado town provides the following services to his patients. [1]

- Concierge taxi service for patients who don't drive
- Umbrella escort for patients to and from the door when it's raining or snowing
- No waiting (He gives any patient who waits more than 5 minutes a $25 gas card!)

---

[1] Myler, Larry (2015, October 21). Can a Dentist Improve Your Customers' Experience? ***Forbes***. Retrieved from: https://www.forbes.com.

- Beverage service
- Tempurpedic padded treatment chairs
- *Doctor Fuji* massage chair therapy
- Aromatherapy
- Noise-reducing headphones
- After-treatment hot towel lavage therapy
- A telephone call to every patient the evening after treatment
- His personal cell phone number to call in case there's an emergency

How can he afford to offer services like that?

That's the wrong question.

You should be asking, "How can he afford NOT to?"

See, it used to be that all a dentist had to do to survive was identify the patient's source of pain, propose a solution, and provide competent treatment. Dentists assumed that as long as they provided competent treatment, patient loyalty was a given. That led to complacency – going through the motions of practicing dentistry, without giving a second thought to the customer experience. After all, the patients would just keep coming back.

Not anymore.

As technology has advanced, and as more people have entered the profession and opened independent practices, the market has become saturated. What does that mean to you?

It means you've got competition. It means you can't assume patient loyalty. You have to create it by proving you value your patients more than the practice down the street. If you don't, the patients you assume are loyal to you and your practice will find someone else to treat them.

And it means that there's quite literally a race. Every practice that raises the bar on its own patient care is raising patient expectations for every dental practice in town – including yours.

If you aren't focusing your practice on *Customer Experience,* or CX, you might find yourself losing the race, no matter how great your clinical skills.

What is *Customer Experience*?

Customer Experience, or CX, is a current business term used to define and measure the interactions between a company and its customers throughout the duration of their relationship, and how those interactions affect a company's top line.

Here's a story that illustrates why Nordstrom is one of the companies best known for providing shockingly good customer experiences.[2]

---

[2]Conte, Christian. (2012, September 7). Nordstrom customer service tales not just legend. ***Jacksonville Business Journal.*** Retrieved from: http://www.bizjournals.com/jacksonville

A member of Nordstrom's housekeeping staff found a customer's bags along with her receipt and an airline itinerary sitting in the parking lot. The staff member returned to the store and looked up the customer's name in the system, knowing she was on her way to the airport. After several attempts to phone the customer without getting an answer, the staff member drove...with the bags...to JFK airport and had the airline page the customer to tell her the staff member had found the bags and was waiting at the airport to return them to her.

Another well-known story of amazing customer experience occurred in December 2013.[3]

At the check-in counter for a WestJet flight to Calgary, staff directed passengers to a video monitor where a WestJet Santa asked what each of them wanted most for Christmas. Once all 250 passengers had checked in, the WestJet staff went to work, rushing to stores all over Calgary to purchase, wrap, and deliver the requested gifts to baggage claim. When the flight landed in Calgary, passengers were greeted not only with their baggage, but also with the gift each one had requested. Their reactions were caught on film and the videos went viral, cementing WestJet's reputation as a caring, customer-focused company.

---

[3] Bender, Andrew. (2013, December 12). The Real 'Christmas Miracle' Of WestJet's Viral Video: Millions in Free Advertising. **Forbes**. Retrieved from: https://www.forbes.com

Companies like these consistently rank among the highest for customer experience because they don't focus on providing "good" or "acceptable" customer service. **They are committed to providing extraordinary, 5-Star, world-class experiences** to their customers at every touch point in every single interaction. Their customers are not just customers...they are raving fans.

Their employees are outgoing, responsive, and engaged, focused on giving you what you want, not just what you need.

And lest you think that you, as the owner of a mere dental practice, couldn't begin to provide the kind of shockingly amazing customer experiences as well as a huge organization like a high-end department store or an international airline, think again.

Think about the companies that you love to do business with. What makes you love them? Would you like to be one of them?

Think about the Colorado dentist that opened this chapter.

Chances are you love to do business with companies who value you as a person, treat you like your business is important, and anticipate your needs before you even ask. You love to do business with companies that delight you.

If you want your practice not just to survive but to thrive, if you want a practice full of delighted patients, and a team committed to providing the kind of service that makes your patient experience special, you must create it!

Before we discuss exactly how to go about creating that kind of practice, let's examine the foundation of Patient Experience.

8 Fundamentals of Patient Experience

1. Every interaction creates a personal reaction.
Realize that every interaction between a patient and your team creates one of two reactions: positive or negative. Your patients' reactions will determine the health of your practice.

World-class companies are obsessed about doing whatever they can to ensure their customers have positive experiences. They recognize, however, that experience is unique to every person and every situation, and therefore they understand the importance of making every experience a personal one.

After all, experiences designed for everyone pleases no one. Too often, we become complacent, just going through the motions, losing sight of our patients as individuals while we go about the technical aspects of our job. And nobody wants to be invisible.

2. People are instinctively self-centered.
All too often, we approach and interact with our

patients from our own business or policy perspective. We don't take into account that every human being has his or her own frame of reference, and cares intensely about their own needs and desires above all else.

Think about the last time you ran late, for example. Even though you had a perfectly valid reason, your patient became irritated (justifiably so). Explaining your reason for the inconvenience didn't change the fact that your patient was inconvenienced and it didn't do anything to decrease their irritation. Likewise, although you and your team understand and speak "dental," your patients might not understand the complexities of that language, and as a result might not experience a connection with you or your team.

The challenge is to interact with patients from *their* model of the world, not yours.

3. Knowing your patients as individuals creates a better patient experience.

Knowing your individual patients, their likes and dislikes, their needs and wants, what makes them happy, and what disappoints them or makes them uncomfortable can help align decisions, plan strategies, and create a better experience all around.

Empowering your team at every level to ask the kinds of questions that reveal the quality of the patient experience will help you begin to offer the kind of world-class service that will set your practice apart from the competition.

4. Unengaged employees create unengaged patients.

Employees with low morale cannot "wow" anybody.

A recent Gallup [4] poll showed that only 32% of the U.S workforce is truly engaged at work. Why should you care? Employee engagement directly affects your profit. To illustrate, Best Buy found that for every one-tenth-of-a-point increase in employee engagement, each Best Buy store increased profits by an amazing $100,000 a year.

To improve patient experience, make it a goal to provide "5-Star Service," and then manage and engage your employees to support the effort.

To paraphrase a 2008 article from *Harvard Business Review*, [5]"Profit and growth are simulated primarily by patient' loyalty. Loyalty is a direct result of patient' satisfaction. Satisfaction is largely influenced by the value of service provided to patients.

---

[4] Mann, Annamarie, and Harter, Jim. (2016, January 7). The Worldwide Employee Engagement Crisis **Gallup**. Retrieved from: http://www.gallup.com/businessjournal

[5] Heskett, J., Jones, T.O., Loverman, G.W., Sasser, E., Schlesinger, L.A. (2008, July-August). Putting the Service-Profit Chain to Work. **Harvard Business Review.** Retrieved from: https://hbr.org

' **Value is created by satisfied, loyal, and productive employees**."

Be aware that you can't just change your business rules and processes and assume that your staff will serve your patients better. Your team will need help to shift their behavior and your culture to make the changes that will transform your practice.

5. Employees do what you measure, incentivize, and celebrate.

How will you know when you have improved your customer experience? A basic tenet of business is that you cannot expect to improve what you haven't measured. Therefore, you must put systems in place to measure the effectiveness of every touchpoint in your patient's experience of your practice, track the numbers, and reward your employees for reaching them. What should you measure? The short answer is "everything:"

a. Number of rings before the telephone is answered; time spent on "hold"

b. Average time in the waiting room/reception area

c. Number of missed and late-cancelled appointments

d. Hygiene retention

e. Acceptance rate of treatment by provider

f. (You get the idea)

Once you have created measurement systems for each position on your team, some team members will improve just by tracking their own numbers. If you add incentives and link salary and/or bonus to improved performance numbers and patient feedback, your team members will have the chance to grow from the minor leagues to the A team because they understand what the game actually is.

6. Make a 5-Star Patient Experience the top priority for you and your team.

You can't fake a commitment to outstanding customer experience.

You and every single member of your team must be obsessively committed to the goal of providing superior service – otherwise, it will be difficult to achieve it. That means each team member must be empowered to recognize opportunities to exceed your patients' expectations.

Aligning as a team to provide exceptional service means that each team member lets patients know how important they are. Each team member shows respect for patients' time, money, circumstances, and effort. Each team member is bold and direct in asking questions, listening to answers, and communicating effectively when handing the patient off to the next team member. Each team member recognizes, at each touchpoint in the treatment process, that he or she can offer personal attention and service beyond the norm. Each team member notes and hands off the information effectively.

Most important, each team member must have permission to offer patients something to rave about to their family, friends, neighbors and business associates.

7. Make sure you have the right people in the right positions on your team.

It may seem obvious, but turning your team into a high performing, patient-centered, well-oiled machine starts by making sure you match responsibilities with skill-sets. After all, it doesn't matter how big the goal is, if you're plagued with a grumpy receptionist or scatter-brained assistant, you can't expect to provide quality patient experience.

Look carefully at each team position and at each touchpoint in your patient care. In addition to professional skills required, look at the "intangible," personality types that would best perform in those positions.

> Front office staff needs to be warm, friendly, happy, and outgoing. The person who answers your phone must have a pleasant, animated voice and excellent phone etiquette. They are your "sunshine" personality. The team member who manages your social media accounts must be

conscientious, reliable, organized, and possess excellent communication skills. Your accounts receivables manager must be accurate, reliable, and compassionate when dealing with patients.

8. Be the leader your team wants to follow and the dentist patients demand to see.

We've saved the most important for last: You must lead by example.

If your intention is to transform your practice and provide outstanding patient experiences, you must commit to making it your top priority and walk the walk. If you just give lip service to transforming your patient experience without follow-through, your team will not engage with you and your efforts will fail quickly.

Everything about your demeanor at work speaks volumes to your team about how to treat your patients. Treat your patients the way you want your team to treat them. Your tone of voice, the words you use, your body language, and the way you conduct yourself in every action throughout your day, influence not just team performance – it influences the entire patient experience, in turn, the success of your practice.

Involve your team in creating ideal new patient strategies. Recognize and reward personal initiative as a way to encourage your team to provide the best patient experiences they can. Use mistakes or crucial feedback as opportunities to learn and grow.

Celebrate your progress.

And keep moving forward!

Ideas for Action: How to Create a Stellar Patient Experience in Your Practice

1. **Begin with the end in mind**.
   Imagine what your practice would look like if it were achieving excellence (You might even want to engage your team in this as a brainstorming exercise). How do you and your team feel about showing up at work on an average Monday morning? How many patients would you see each day? How do your patients feel when you greet them at the front desk...in the treatment room...when leaving the office? How many referrals or new patients could you count on each week? What would be the prevailing "mood" in the office? What would your accounts receivable look like? Be as specific as you can – after all, right now it's just an ideal.

2. **Take stock of where you are right now, relative to your idea of "the perfect practice."**
   If you don't know where you are right now, you won't know when you have made any progress. That's why it's important to acknowledge reality and tell the truth about your practice as it is right now. Ask yourself (and your team) the following questions:
   - How well do we communicate with our patients from the first call to the care call after the last visit? Is our communication system consistent

from team member to team member, patient to patient?
- What is the average waiting time to get an appointment? To be seen once a patient arrives for their appointment?
- Do our patients give us any concrete, specific feedback about their experience with us? Do we even ask them for feedback? Do we thank them for their business?
- What action do we take as a team— if at all – to discuss, revise, and improve our policies or protocols based on a patient's dissatisfaction or complaint?
- What, specifically, are we currently doing to go above and beyond to provide a superior patient experience?
- How many referrals are we getting from our existing patients?
- What is the status of our accounts receivable?
- How much profit/loss are we experiencing?
- What is our current level of growth?

Any surprising or painful answers you discover in this exercise are opportunities. They provide the insight that will challenge you to innovate, change, and grow. They will reveal the strategy required to move your practice closer to your vision. And remember, innovation, change, and growth will require you to embody the adaptable mindset we discussed in Chapter 2.

3. Formally ask your patients for concrete, specific feedback.

Savvy dentists and practice managers realize that patient feedback can quite literally mean money in the bank. But many others are fearful of hearing complaints, dealing with dissatisfaction, and handling uncomfortable "bad news." Again, you must adapt. It might help to consider feedback as nothing more than a request: negative feedback is a request to do something differently and become the hero; positive feedback is a request to keep doing more of what you are currently doing.

Design a feedback mechanism for your patients. Let them know how important they are to you, and tell them you are on a mission to transform your practice and provide exceptional patient experiences, and ask them to help you by providing concrete, specific examples of what you are doing right, what you could do better, and what would delight them about your practice. Ask them in person. Design a feedback form they can complete on site or email back to you. Call them after an appointment. Set up an online survey (you can do it at no cost) and email your patients the link to the survey.

Again, you can't change what you don't measure. Feedback is a way for you to highlight your strengths and pinpoint your areas for improvement.

LET US HELP YOU!

You're a busy Doctor, with lots on your plate. If the idea of implementing anything in this chapter seems overwhelming to you, we have your solutions.

We're here to help.

Call us or visit our website at
www.dmicoaching.com

Chapter 5:

How to Create Rapport with Anyone in 30 Seconds or Less

"To effectively communicate, we must realize that we are all different in the way we perceive the world and use this understanding as a guide to our communication with others." – Tony Robbins

Have you ever met a total stranger and immediately felt as though you've known that person for years? You felt at ease and comfortable in that person's presence. Talking and listening seemed effortless. You simply felt good around them.

What you experienced is *rapport*.

Rap·port *(/raˈpôr/ Noun: a close and harmonious relationship in which the people or groups concerned understand each other's feelings or ideas and communicate well.*

When you experience rapport with someone, it's as if you've entered their world, see things from their perspective, feel how they are feeling, and understand where they are coming from. Rapport is what allows you to interact with others in a way that creates trust and understanding from your very first interaction, whether over the phone or face-to-face. It is the ability to see and understand a person's point of view and guide them to understand yours.

In other words, quite simply, rapport is connecting with someone on an emotional level.

Why is rapport important to you, as a dental professional and business owner?

When you experience rapport with your patients, they feel good in your presence. They feel listened to. They feel understood. Feeling good, feeling heard and understood in your presence, they will be more open to your suggestions.

When you experience rapport with your team, it makes everyday decision-making and cooperation much more effective.

Getting your patients to accept your suggestions, willingly agree to proposed treatment plans, and make better decisions about their own oral health is the very foundation of a thriving, healthy dental practice, and must be the core focus of a well-functioning treatment team.

Whether you are comfortable with it or not, the fact is that you, as the practice owner and treatment expert, are trying to sell something. You are selling the treatment plans you propose to your patients. You are selling your management systems and processes to your staff. Whether or not you can successfully get your patients and your team to buy what you're selling depends entirely on your ability to create rapport.

Many practices struggle along, frustrated with uncooperative team and patients who waffle about accepting recommended treatment plans. These practices might just be the ones who try to dazzle their patients with the sound logic of why the treatment is necessary. They list all of the "good reasons" the staff should adopt new systems or procedures. They fail to understand one simple, brutal fact:

People buy products and services based on *EMOTIONS*, and then rationalize those decisions with logic. They base buying decisions on "feeling," not "thinking."

In other words, people buy something because they **want** it, not because they need it.

Successful practices know how to reach their patients emotionally as well as logically. They know how to trigger the "I want" button to shift patients quickly into a buying state of mind first; then they provide the logical reasons that help the patients justify their buying decision.

We'll discuss the sales aspect of your practice in more detail in the following chapters. For now, it's important to realize that successful practitioners are those who master and learn the skills required to create instant rapport.

So how do you create this mystical, "magical" state of rapport?

Let's look first at how human minds work.

What are you focused on, right this minute?

You might be aware of reading these words, moving your eyes along the page, the quality of your breathing, the light in the room, the noise outside, your stomach rumbling, the music on the radio. You might even be focusing on all of these things, now that you're aware of them.

That's your **conscious** mind right there. It's what's in your awareness.

Your conscious mind is your logical and digital processor. It constantly questions whether something is true or false, rational or irrational. Your conscious mind is linear, logical, and sequential and wants everything to make sense.

To illustrate, recall learning to drive. You had to focus on many things, in logical sequential order: *"check your mirrors...put on the turn signal...right foot gas and brake, left foot clutch...check your speed...keep three car lengths behind the car in front of you...watch for pedestrians...maintain your cool if you see a police car behind you...uh oh, 4-way stop...his turn, her turn, now it's my turn..."*

Your conscious mind, able to process and manage between five and nine "chunks" of data every second, was in charge of driving while you learned.

But ask yourself this: have you ever pulled into your driveway and been completely unaware of driving there? Driving is now automatic to you. It's a habit. Your ***unconscious*** mind is now doing pretty much all of the driving.

Capable of processing millions of bits of data every second, your unconscious mind processes and stores your experiences and memories as images, sounds, and feelings. Under the surface, automatically, your unconscious mind manages all of your bodily functions (breathing, heartbeat, blood flow, reflexes, and so forth), as well as storing and organizing your beliefs, values, and habits. Its job is to protect you from harm and help you survive.

Everything you see, hear, and feel, even if you imagine it, dream it, or watch it on film, is real to your unconscious mind. The unconscious mind is incapable of distinguishing fact from fiction, real from imagined, personal from impersonal. Case in point: have you ever jumped out of your seat while watching a scary movie?

Like a small child, your unconscious mind wants to serve and protect you, but it needs clear direction to do what you want it to do.

Think of the relationship between your conscious mind and unconscious mind like this: the captain of a ship (conscious mind), surveys the ocean, gives orders and corrects the course from the bridge based on the ship's intended destination. Below decks, in the engine room, the crew (unconscious mind) carries out the captain's orders according to their years of training (habit).

Cognitive neuroscientists have concluded that the unconscious mind accounts for well over 90% of brain function, and commonly use the iceberg metaphor to help understand the functions and relationship between them.

"An enormous portion of cognitive activity is non-conscious, figuratively speaking, it could be 99 percent; we probably will never know precisely how much is outside awareness."[6] (Dr. Emmanuel Donchin, Distinguished Professor of uroscience, University of South Florida).

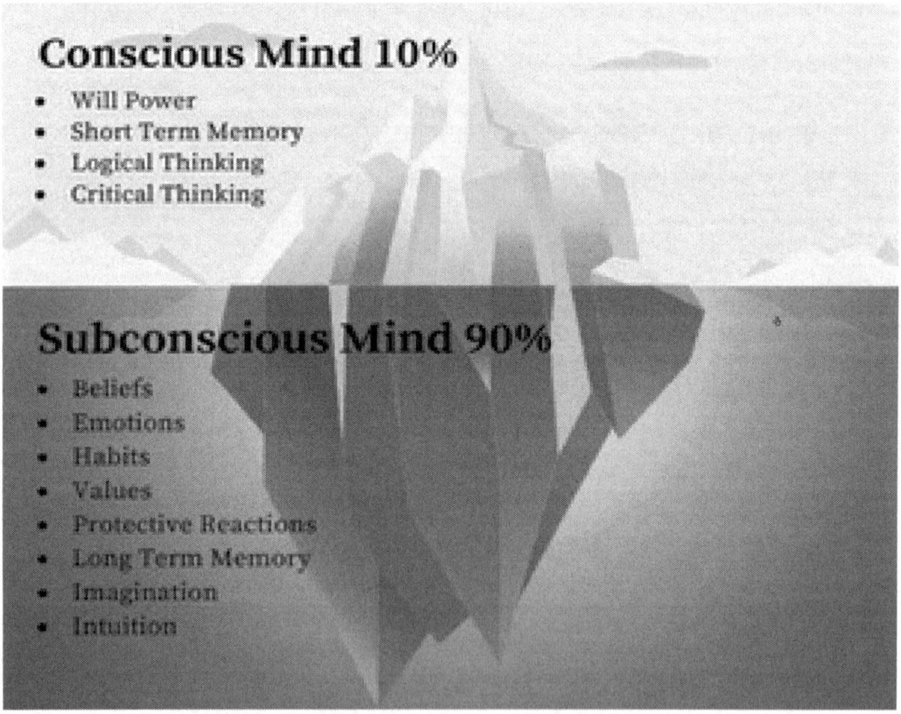

---

[6]Goleman, Daniel. (1984, February 7). New View of Mind Gives Unconscious an Expanded Role. *New York Times*. Retrieved from: http://www.nytimes.com/

Understanding how the mind works helps us understand how to create rapport.

Since the ***conscious*** mind is linear, sequential, and logical, you might say it is responsible for the words you use to communicate. If you're "telling" people things to try to engage, influence, or persuade them, you're not using all of the tools at your disposal.

The unconscious mind, on the other hand, is emotional. If what we want to do is establish rapport, that state of emotional safety and closeness, we need to look under the surface at the ***unconscious*** mind and how it influences our communication.

How do We Communicate?

The science of *kinesics* is based on the fact that to communicate, human beings need and use all of their senses to convey information -- not just words. Gestures, facial expressions, tonality and movement convey far more than our words. These "unconscious" aspects of communication convey our emotional state, our beliefs, values, opinions, and desires. All human cultures encode patterns of gestures, facial expressions, and other physical movements to carry information. Studying these patterns can reveal the code and convey the meaning intended within given social settings.

Dr. Ray Birdwhisttell, a pioneer in of *kinesics*, conducted a study at the University of Pennsylvania and concluded that **93%** of our communication happens non-verbally. More than half, **55%,** of our message is delivered by our physiology (our body language), **38%** is carried in the tonality (how we say our words), and only **7%** of our message is delivered by the words we choose to speak.[7]

In other words, the majority of our communication is *unconscious*!

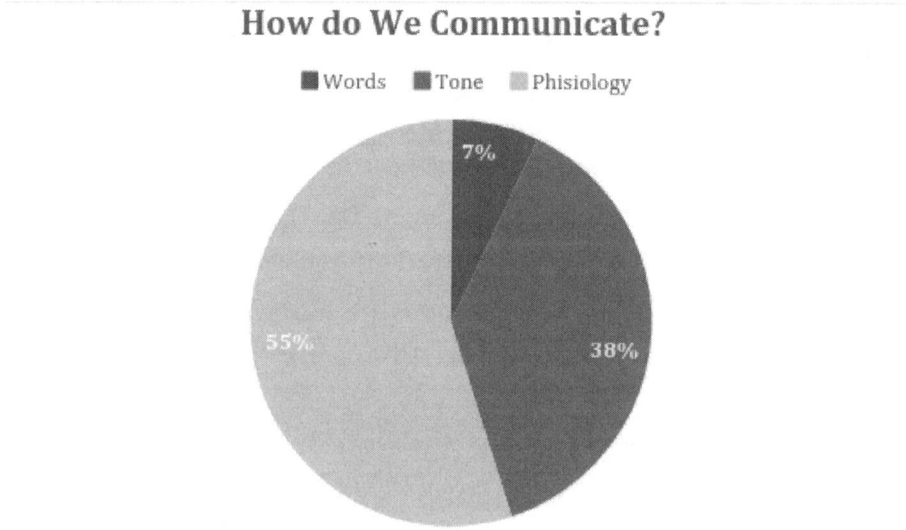

[7] Birdwhitsell, Dr. Ray. (1970). *Kinesics and Context Essays on Body Motion Communication.* Philadelphia, PA. University of Pennsylvania Press

To create rapport, we must learn to master the unconscious "code" used by the people we're trying to communicate with. And if we want to influence or persuade people, we have to understand where they are coming from, so we can guide them to accept our desired outcome.

In simple terms, you must meet the person at their starting line so you can gracefully lead them to your desired finish line.

First, we have to train ourselves to see the starting line, by observing how people communicate with themselves and with others.

Building rapport requires attention, or *conscious* awareness.

Four Preferred Communication Styles

Each person prefers a particular way to learn and exchange information. That preference is driven by the person's ***unconscious*** mind, and is revealed not only by the words they use, but also by their nonverbal behaviors. Some people prefer to learn and communicate by seeing...some by touching...some by hearing...and some by processing or thinking digitally.

Listen to the way you communicate, and the ways people around you communicate. Do you hear things like, "I see what you mean," or, "That rings a bell," or,

"I feel like a burger tonight"? These phrases tend to reveal preferred communication styles. As we discussed, the ***unconscious*** mind helps us process information through our senses (sight, sound, touch, smell, and taste, for example). We then build our particular model of the world based on the experiences we perceive and the language, emotion, and sensations we attach to those experiences.

Let's look specifically at four preferred communication styles or learning modalities: *Visual*, *Auditory*, *Kinesthetic*, and *Auditory Digital*. The following charts can help you become aware (***conscious***) and "decode" not only your own preferences, but those of your team and your patients as well. The degree to which you can become ***conscious*** of a person's preferred way to send and receive information is the degree to which you can truly establish rapport.

Visual	
• Organized, neat, well-groomed • Speak quickly • Breath higher in chest • Speak more slowly than visuals • Fewer voice inflections • Want to be shown concepts • Prefer visual descriptions • Prefer to see a picture of what you are saying • Prefer to see people's reactions • Memorize by visual association • Would prefer to read than be read to • Use arms to gesture and make more facial expressions • Prefer pictures, x-rays, models, imaging, drawings	• Use visualization for memory • Use visualization to make decisions • Imaginative and tend to have difficulty putting ideas to words • May get confused by long, verbal instruction • Prefer demonstrations than speeches • Difficulty concentrating with visual distractions • Remember faces rather than names • Tend to be spontaneous • Interrupt others

Kinesthetic	
• Tend to speak slowly • More sensitive to their bodies • More sensitive to their feelings • Respond to physical rewards and touching • Touch people to get their attention • Tend to stand close to others when speaking with them • Can have challenges with traditional education	• Learn by touching, moving and doing • Dress and groom themselves for comfort • Make decisions based on feelings • Feel emotions deeply • Responsive to soft touch, tenderness, temperature, and pain • Are less interested in pictures and images, preferring to touch and feel models
Auditory	
• Tend to speak at a medium pace • Aware of subtle changes in tone of voice • Learn by listening and asking questions • remember what is discussed rather than seen • Prefer to communicate through spoken language rather than	• Need to be heard by others • Talk problems through and like to use others as sounding boards for them • Easily distracted by noise • Follow verbal directions • Talk to themselves while working • Speak in rhythmic patterns • Move their lips while

written word • Enjoy listening to music, conversation and silence	reading • Can mimic tone, pitch and timbre
Auditory Digital (AD)	
• Have to make sense of things • Need to figure things out to understand them • Learn by working it out in their minds • Use internal dialogue to make sense of their world • Like to think, plan and analyze • Use less animated facial expressions and body gestures • Like predictability	• Prefer lists, sequences, flow charts, facts and figures • Good at categorizing and summarizing • Like to think things through logically before making decisions • May do or say the same thing over and over • Need to understand why • something is important • Very organized • Prefer to be right, precise and accurate

In addition to the non-verbal characteristics of each style charted above, the words a person uses will help you more clearly understand their preferred communication modality. Here are some examples of language that can help you decode a person's preferred communication modality.

Key Words and Metaphors for Each Modality			
Visual	**Auditory**	**Kinesthetic**	**Auditory Digital**
See Look Picture Imagine Show Focus Appear View Reveal Envision Tunnel Vision Illuminate Bright Vivid See eye to eye It's clear/not clear Take a look at I see what you mean Clear as day Try to see things my way	Hear Tell Listen Sound Tune in Tune out Rings a bell All ears Clear as a bell Be heard Resonate Rings a bell Silence Announce Tune into this I hear you Sounds good I hear what you are saying We speak the same language Loss for words	Feel Grasp Touch Catch on Concrete Get a handle Catch on Solid Get hold of Tap Into Impression Sensation Hard Unfeeling I feel like Get a grip on One step at a time Rubs me the wrong way Maintain a sense of balance A cool customer	Process Think Know Process Experience Understand Sense Decide Consider Perceive Question Describe Motivate Change Makes sense That's logical Without a doubt I can't figure this out Let me process this for a minute I know that

To reiterate, becoming conscious of your patient's preferred form of communication is essential to creating rapport and discussing necessary treatment. And knowing the preferred communication styles of each person on your team, will help you develop greater rapport with them, and help them willingly cooperate and support you.

When you start communicating based on your patient's model of the world (or anyone else's, for that matter), rather than projecting your own model of the world onto them, they will be far more understanding and open to your suggestions. It will also help you understand what's behind their complaints or objections, as well as aid you in helping them understand what you are trying to communicate to them.

How to Show Your Patient you Truly Understand Them

There's an old Zen saying: *"It's easier to ride the horse in the direction it's going."*

In other words, to ensure mutual understanding, it's more effective to communicate using your patient's preferred model, instead of coming from your own.

Or, as Anthony Robbins said,

"People who are ***like*** *each other tend to* ***like*** *each other."*

People cooperate more willingly with those they like and trust. Mirroring, matching, and pacing, help you become "like" the others with whom you want to establish rapport, and will help them like and trust you in return.

Mirroring, Matching and Pacing

Mirroring, matching, or pacing all describe the subtle action of reflecting someone's behavior back to them by displaying that behavior yourself, as if you're falling into step with them and entering their model of the world.

Pay attention to everything they are communicating. Look at their physiology. Listen to their voice. Pay attention to the words and language they are using, and reflect it back to them:

Physiology	Tonality	Language
• Posture • Hand Gestures • Facial Expressions • Spinal Alignment • Head Tilt • Blinking • Breathing Rate • Energy	• Tone (Pitch) • Tempo (Speed) • Timbre (Quality) • Volume (Loudness/Quietn ess)	• Predicates • Key Words • Common Experiences • Content Chunk (Amount of words used)

Here's how:

If a patient gestures broadly with their hands, you want to add more gestures when you're communicating. If they are smiling, smile back. If they are talking at three times the speed of light, speed up your own speech. If they are using phrases that indicate one of the four modalities (for example, "I don't see what you mean," "That doesn't sound like something I'd like to do," or "It feels like this might be expensive"), use those modalities in your own language. If they're speaking softly, speak quietly yourself. Repeat to the patient exactly what you heard them say, using their words. In other words, **be like** the person who's communicating with you.

Mirroring, matching, and pacing demonstrates very clearly to your patients that you understand them. And when people (particularly your patients and your team) feel understood, they are more likely to comply with your instructions, follow your treatment plans, and make better decisions.

Learning to create genuine rapport will quite literally transform your relationships with your team, with your patients, and with virtually any person in your life and it is like learning any new skill.

At first, it will remind you of learning to drive, or learning to swim, or learning to seat a crown properly. You'll have to talk yourself through it, ***conscious*** at every step until it becomes a habit.

Ideas for Action: Become Conscious of Communication Modalities, and Create Rapport with Anyone...in 30 Seconds or Less

1. Train yourself to recognize a person's preferred communication style. Conduct your own research: spend a few minutes each day observing the people around you (your family, your team, your patients, the businesspeople you encounter) and note how they communicate. Listen for the verbal cues that reveal their preferred style. Watch their body language – posture, gestures, and facial expressions. Listen to the speed, tone, and volume of their speech. Practice becoming aware of these clues.

2. Practice mirroring, matching and pacing. When you're ordering your morning latte, picking up your clothes at the dry cleaner, or chatting with the neighbor, make a conscious effort to mirror their posture, gestures, tone, volume, pitch, and echo the words and phrases they use. Note any differences in the quality of your interaction.

3. As a team-building exercise, conduct a communication styles inventory with your entire team. You can find a free assessment on our website at **www.dmicoaching.com**. Once they're complete, have your team share their results with

one another, and create an action plan to implement what you learn

In the next chapter, we'll examine the importance of rapport in designing an impactful new patient interview, and guiding your existing patients to accept the treatment plans you feel would be best for them.

Contact us at www.dmicoaching.com for assistance

Chapter 6

Your Practice is not About You, It's About Your Patients

What is Your "Big Why?"

Why did you choose to become a dentist?

Was it the prestige? The money? The freedom of being your own boss, setting your own hours, becoming financially comfortable while charging whatever you want for your services?

After all, yours is a stressful profession. Your job demands perfection, as you work with powerful, expensive equipment in a tiny, restricted workspace, on people who are nervous, anxious, or downright scared to have you poking around in their mouths. Many patients are fearful of the cost of treatment. They don't follow your directions, won't accept your proposed treatment plans, and are slow to pay their bills.

And the team? It can be a challenge to put together and manage a team that truly supports you. You have to take on hiring, training, motivating, supervising, and providing salary and benefits. They call in sick. They show up late. They don't seem to care. Or worse, they just seem to go through the motions to collect a paycheck.

And the expense! The costs of paying off student loans, maintaining an office, keeping current with technological advances, buying and maintaining modern equipment, and working with sometimes convoluted insurance regulations can be staggering, leaving you to enjoy only a small percentage of your leftover revenue as profit.

Seriously, why? Why in the world would you choose to submit yourself willingly to that kind of stress?

If you find yourself feeling stressed, de-motivated, or depressed about your chosen career, look deeper at your reasons for choosing it.

Chances are there was something else – something much bigger and more noble – that motivated your career choice, gets you up to go to work each day, and powers you through the stress.

Perhaps you want to be of service to people. Perhaps you find joy in solving intricate problems, or in working with precision to help people look and feel better. Perhaps you love restoring function or creating beauty. Perhaps you feel a deep calling to relieve people's pain and suffering. That's why you chose to become a dentist.

Because you want to accomplish all of those things, you make a diagnosis and recommend a course of treatment. After all, most clinicians do just that. They want to make a difference, so they try to convince their patients to do what's best.

In other words, the dentist assumes that the **patient needs** what the **dentist wants** to do.

If you want to experience the deep satisfaction of providing that kind of service, if you want to transform your practice so that your team runs like a well-oiled machine and your patients rave about you and provide a steady stream of referrals, you must shift your focus and realize:

Your patients only care about what THEY want.

You must understand that your practice is not about you. It's about them.

What is Their "Big Why?"

Now ask yourself this question, and see if you can dig deep for the answers.

Why do your patients come to see you?

After all, a morning at the dentist is not as much fun as a night out on the town, or as relaxing as an afternoon at the ball game. There's pain. There's waiting. There's apprehension, anxiety, or fear. There's discomfort, as somebody in a white lab coat and protective goggles pokes their gloved hands and shoves instruments around inside their mouths. There's a conversation over them, in a language they might not understand. There's noise and smells. There are weird sensations of pressure, vibration, taste, numbness, and a mouthful of water. And then there's the expense...and a free toothbrush at the end.

Why on earth would people subject themselves to all of that?

Because they want something that makes all of that discomfort worth it.

Your job is to help your patients understand that you can help them get it. Getting your patients to realize you can help them get what they most deeply want, demands you develop and perfect two skills: *influence* and *persuasion*.

In the last chapter, we discussed the importance of establishing rapport, the feeling of almost immediate connection that communicates a shared worldview with another person. The next step is to build on the rapport you have established so you can influence and persuade the patient that you are there to help them get what they want.

To influence or persuade your patients to willingly accept treatment, you first have to know what it is that they want.

That requires a shift in your focus. You must grab the reins of the dentist/patient relationship, and manage the way your patients see you.

How Do Your Patients See You?

How many times has a patient responded to your recommended treatment plan by saying something like this?

> *"Well, I need to check my schedule," I'll get back to you," "Let me check with my spouse" or "It just costs too much and I can't afford it right now."*

How do you respond?

Do you see their response as an obstacle you have to overcome? After all, your years of education and experience tell you that this patient **needs** what you are recommending, and just doesn't "get it." They just don't understand the logic of getting their dental problems fixed right now, the right way. After all, you can provide financing options. The treatment won't hurt them. You're the best in your community at providing exactly what they need. Why don't they get that? Why don't they say "Yes"?

Let's be brutally honest here. Of course they can't see it…yet. They're incapable of understanding it and making a decision right now. Why?

Because your patients make decisions emotionally and then justify their decisions with logic.

If your patients are responding to you with that kind of reluctance, with those sorts of "objections," it simply means you haven't connected with them emotionally. And without that emotional connection, you are in no position to try to influence or persuade them of anything.

The first step to making that emotional connection requires that you acknowledge your role (and your relationship) from Their point of view. You're the dentist. They're the patient. What does the dentist/patient relationship look like to them?

What do they think of dentists? What did they like and dislike about their previous dentist? Have they been putting off treatment? Why? Are they nervous? Afraid to trust you because of bad or painful experiences by other dentists? Are they worried about the costs and time involved in treatment?

Are you just some scary, clinical, white-coated, loop-wearing, gloved-handed sadist who's going to poke, prod, cause them pain, and then charge them loads of money for the privilege? Why should they trust you?

Successful clinicians and managers are those who have mastered the ability to manage their relationships by shifting the way their patients perceive the doctor/patient relationship.

Instead of hearing those responses as obstacles or objections, successful doctors use them as opportunities to show patients a new possibility. From that perspective, they are better able to influence and persuade their patients to step into that new possibility.

To make that shift, you want to take charge of the relationship, and transform the way your patients experience you.

Manage the Way Your Patient Sees You

Imagine this scenario:

> *Taylor, your first patient, was extremely nervous and agitated, had difficulty getting and staying numb, felt every spin of the drill and verbalized, quite loudly, the pain she was feeling throughout the entire procedure. What was supposed to be a simple crown prep and filling, ended up turning into an hour and a half, 3 surface filling. A loss of $1200 because her crown had to be rescheduled to another day.*

> *You're frustrated, maybe even a little disappointed with yourself because you got impatient with her. Meanwhile, in your reception area, your new patient, Ally, overhears the commotion coming from the treatment room while she fills out her paperwork. You usher your first patient out, then turn and greet your new patient only to recognize fear in her eyes.*

How are you going to manage this new relationship when you still have the stress and negativity of your first patient affecting you and your team? If you don't manage the emotional state you are in, and fast, it will show up in your next interaction, with your next patient.

The secret is to take a deep breath, shift your focus, and **enter her world**, where she is, right now. How might she be feeling? What is she thinking as she sits there? What does she want most? Is she even interested in sticking around after hearing the last patient's reaction? How can you let her know – immediately – that she can trust you?

To create immediate rapport with this new patient, you're going to have to manage not only your own emotional state, but hers as well. You're going to have to **interrupt and shift the way your patient might be seeing and experiencing you**.

How?

Become aware and **communicate consciously**. Take command of the relationship with confident body language, a reassuring tone of voice, and the words you use to communicate with her. A warm smile, direct eye contact, an extended hand, getting knee to knee, all intended to reassure the patient you are there to support her and treat her well, can trigger your patient to change the way she feels about you.

Mirroring, matching, and pacing (as we discussed in the last chapter) will powerfully communicate to your patients that you recognize, appreciate and understand how they see and experience you, your team and your practice.

Before you even begin the exam or treatment presentation, you must take the time to discover who your patient is, what drives them, what interests them, what is important to them by asking questions and expressing sincere interest in the answers. An effective patient interview can help get you those answers, and we'll focus on that process in the next chapter.

For now, it's important to realize that one of the biggest mistakes clinicians make is to begin an exam or treatment presentation without ever establishing the necessary rapport. Clinicians fail to realize that their patient does not care about them or their interests. And failing to establish rapport, failing to recognize the patient's interests, values and desires, can hamper any efforts to exert influence or persuade your patient to accept treatment.

Help Your Patients See You as a Solution to Their Problem

Getting your patients to see you as a solution and agree to a treatment plan will require you to get to the bottom of what the patient truly wants by exploring their core emotional needs. Getting the information that will help you understand their wants and needs requires that you develop three skills:

1. Rapport
2. Influence
3. Persuasion

We've discussed how to create rapport – that feeling of immediate closeness -- in some depth. And in the next chapter, we'll explore in detail how to develop a patient interview process that will help you deepen your understanding of your patient's wants and needs and explore together how you can meet them.

First, though, it's important to understand the fundamentals of persuasion and influence, and their role in getting your patients to "yes" as quickly as possible, so you can do what you do best with the passion and integrity that drove you into this profession in the first place.

> ***Persuasion:***
> *Process aimed at changing a person's (or a group's) attitude or behavior toward some event, idea, object, or other person(s), by* ***using written or spoken words to convey information, feelings, or reasoning, or a combination of them***[8]*.*

Again, people buy what they **WANT**, not what they **need**. And **they buy for emotional reasons, and then use logic to justify their decisions**. You, as a dental professional, are trained to know what your patients need, and why they need it.

But your good, sound, professionally based reasons by themselves will not move your patients to accept treatment. Telling them what they need will not persuade them.

You must show them and explain how and why the treatment you offer helps them get what they WANT.

In other words, persuasion is the art of getting people to do things for their OWN reasons, not yours. It requires that you get patients to clearly associate their most desired feelings, those things

---

[8]Persuasion. Business Dictionary.com. Retrieved June 09, 2017, from BusinessDictionary.com website:http://www.businessdictionary.com/definition/persuasion.htm.

they most deeply want, to the service you can provide.

Basic human psychology teaches us that effective persuasion is a balancing act between two emotional states: **pain or pleasure**. People are motivated to do something based on either the pleasure they will experience or the pain they will avoid.

Think about the sense of pride that comes from driving a brand new sports car, carrying a designer handbag, feeling beautiful when you smile at yourself in the mirror – all of these are examples of deciding in favor of pleasure. On the other hand, spending more money than you had planned, thoughts of wastefulness, feeling unattractive, feelings of frustration, and avoiding discomfort all illustrate the kind of pain that might be a motivating factor as well.

And people are motivated by different things: not everyone is motivated by the same pleasure or pain.

Persuasion rests on your ability to **help your patient understand there is more pleasure in taking action, and more pain in not acting**. To persuade someone to act, you must help them understand that **where they are now is more painful than where they could be**. You must help them realize that they are dissatisfied with the way things are right now, and that dissatisfaction is much more painful than any concern they may express about the time or money your treatment represents.

Your goal, then, in becoming more effective at persuading your patients to accept treatment is going to require you to explore with them what their primary motivating factors are. Guide them to the point where they realize they are dissatisfied with the way things are now, and show them it will be more pleasurable to take action.

To achieve that goal, you are going to have to know your patients better than they know themselves.

- What is important to them?
- What do they value?
- What motivates them to make a decision?
- What compels them to take action?
- What is their "why" to buy or not to buy?

Once you have a sense of your patient's own motivating factors, you will realize, people say yes to what they value, what they see value in and what they desire to have.

> ***Influence:***
> *The act or power of* ***producing an effect without apparent exertion of force*** *or direct exercise of*

[9]Influence. Merriam-Webster.com. Retrieved June 09,2017, from Merriam-Webster.com website: https://www.merriam-webster.com/dictionary/influence

> *command; the power or capacity of causing an effect in indirect or intangible ways.*[9]

Your ability to influence your patients is the difference between massive success and major failure.

Once you've discovered your patient's key motivators and proven you really understand them, your patients will actually help you justify why they should accept treatment.

Beyond that, you must demonstrate to them that you are committed to improving their quality of life, that you quite literally have the power and ability to shape their destiny. After all, isn't that what you do?

Rapport, persuasion, and influence work together to create a process to help your patients make a choice:

1. First, developing rapport helps you discover enough about your patient to find out where they hurt. There is something they want that they are not presently experiencing, and not having it is painful for them.

2. Second, persuasion requires asking the kinds of questions that will "disturb" your patient. You want to cause them to feel the emotional costs (pain) associated with continuing to avoid taking action versus the relief they will feel if they act (pleasure). In this part of the process, you are quite literally guiding the patient to **want** a

solution.

3. Third, using your influence, you guide the patient into realizing that **your proposed treatment plan will solve their problem, heal their pain, and give them the pleasure of getting what they most deeply want.**

When you find yourself facing patients who offer objections like those we mentioned earlier, "Well, I need to talk with my spouse," I'll get back to you," or "It just costs too much, I can't afford it right now," all the patient is really telling you is that you haven't discovered what is really holding them back from saying yes.

Essentially, these objections (and others like them) represent most people's dominant reasons for not buying or making a decision: **Fear**. Simply, fear of pain, fear of financial hardship, fear of discomfort, fear the treatment won't work. To help the patient work through that fear, you need to dig deeper into the pain of not taking action. **Ask more questions until the patient has a powerful enough emotional reason to decide to take action.** You do not necessarily need to give them more information.

Once you have explored all of the patient's wants, hopes, wishes, desires, and emotional pains, you can offer logical reasons and more information to help your patient justify taking action now.

The next chapter will show you how to conduct an effective patient interview that gives you all the information you need to help your patients get more of what they want from the treatment plans you propose.

Ideas for Action: How to Help Patients Get what They Want

1. Take some time to consider all of the reasons patients (in general) put off dental treatment or avoid it altogether. Create as long a list as you can. Ask your dental team to contribute to this list. Keep adding to the list as you discover more reasons. Use what you discover to create questions that will help your patients understand the **pain** or discomfort those reasons cause them.

2. Create another list, this one cataloging all of the emotional benefits patients might feel when their dental treatment is complete. Again, ask your team to contribute to this list. Use the list to generate questions that help your patients envision how they might feel **emotionally** once they have accepted your proposed treatment plan.

3. Together with your team, think of examples that illustrate times when someone “sold” you something by helping you understand that the

emotional benefit of making the purchase outweighed the pain of not making the purchase.

Here's an example to get you started:

> A young mother is shopping for a new car, as her old car is frequently in the shop for repairs. She loves that old car, and is reluctant to let it go. She's concerned about the costs of frequent repair, but more concerned about the price of a new car. The sales representative greets her on the lot, asks a few questions, and discovers she is the mother of two small children. He asks her about her them. How old are they? What grade are they in? What are their after-school activities? Does she often drive her children and their friends to the water park or the movies?
>
> He does not ask her about her budget!
>
> Based on their conversation, he can see and feel her most basic, underlying emotional desire: the safety of her children and herself on the road. That's what got her to the car dealership in the first place.
>
> He shows her a model top rated for driver and passenger safety, but it is well outside her initial budget. He shows her a second model offered at a lower price, and shows her data illustrating its safety ratings, while good, are not as high as the first, higher-priced model. He

continues to ask questions about her young children and about how the family uses the car. Based on his astute questions, the young mother realizes the safety of her children is far more important than the difference of a few thousand dollars on the price tag.

Thinking of examples from your own experience, as well as those of your team, will help you realize the basic concept of this chapter: **people buy emotionally, and justify their buying decisions with logic.**

Chapter 7:

The Patient Interview - How to Get to Know Your Patients – and Keep them for Life

A patient walks into a typical, modest dental practice. The receptionist, looking harried, is on the phone and raises one hand in a "just a minute" gesture without even looking at the patient. The phone conversation continues for another two minutes, while the new patient stands there, uncomfortably, waiting at the front desk to be acknowledged.

Once the receptionist finishes the phone call, she looks at the computer screen, saying, "You must be Steve," and without a smile, waves him down the hall to the operatory without even a friendly "good morning."

The dentist, his back turned, mumbles, "Go ahead and have a seat while I review your chart; I'll be with you in just a minute." He puts on his mask, adjusts the light, and says, "Hi, I'm Dr. Dentist, nice to meet you. Let's go ahead and do an exam. Open wide for me." At the end of the exam, Dr. Dentist tells his receptionist, "Megan, can you write up a treatment plan for a root canal and crown?" He turns to Steve, saying, "You need a RCT and Crown on #30. Megan will go over this with you. It was nice to meet you."

Megan hands Steve a treatment plan, "Okay, it looks like you need a root canal and crown. Your cost will be $1800. Would you like to schedule that today?"

And they all wonder at the end of the day why their schedule is not full.

That scene, believe it or not, is not an exaggeration. It happens in every town, every day, in more dental offices than you can imagine.

And that's a shame. The key to transforming a mediocre practice like the example above is to create a truly patient-centered practice.

From the moment a new patient contacts your office until the time the treatment is complete, you and your team must do everything possible to focus on the patient and his or her most important wants and needs. Two of the most fundamental things you and your entire team can do are 1) provide a "Smile Questionnaire" to your new patients before you see them, and 2) conduct thorough, thoughtful patient interviews.

An effective, well-structured patient interview consists of open-ended questions designed to help you and your team:

- establish immediate rapport
- create trust and likeability
- discover how your patient's preferred communication style (how they processes information)
- establish the patient's motivation for seeking dental treatment
- understand your patient's values and model of the world
- determine your patient's buying motivators and strategies

Structure and Flow of an Effective Patient Interview

In an ideal, well-functioning, successful practice, all new patients complete a smile questionnaire, either online or when they first arrive at your office. In this questionnaire, you gather information about the patient (what do you like best about your smile, least about your smile, what did you like most about your previous dentist, what did you like least about your previous dentist, why did you leave your last dentist (so you do not make the same mistake), have you ever had an upsetting experience at a dental office, what is important to you that we discuss today, etc.). These questions give you a place to start as you begin to establish rapport and create trust with your new patients.

When your new patient arrives for their first appointment, your receptionist greets and welcomes the patient by name, verifies and enters all the pertinent information from the new patient paperwork and questionnaire into the computer, and introduces the new patient to your treatment coordinator and escorts the new patient to a seat in the consultation room. He or she sits, comfortably facing the patient, and begins the patient interview process by looking over the questionnaire, asking a series of open-ended questions, listening carefully, and taking notes as your patient answers.

As the interview progresses, and as the patient answers, the relationship begins to build. Rapport deepens. The patient becomes more comfortable, and your treatment coordinator can begin to ask deeper questions designed to reveal more intimate information.

The whole point of this process is to gather the information the dentist will need in order to recommend a treatment plan based on what the patient wants, needs, and expects from the practice.

When the treatment coordinator has concluded the interview, he or she hands the resulting notes over to the assistant, hygienist and dentist to review, before meeting the patient for the first time. She will also properly hand the patient off to the clinician verbally reviewing the information gathered.

Ask Questions to Break the Ice and Establish Initial Rapport with Your Patient

The first few questions you want to ask your patient should help your patient feel comfortable and relaxed in your presence. Keep the questions open ended, and let the patient tell you the answers as you observe carefully and take notes. Here are some ideas to help you design your own questions:

- *How did you hear about us?*
- *What brings you here today?*
- *What was the reason for your last visit to the dentist? Did you get what you needed?*
- *What was your experience like?*
- *What are your expectations when you go to the dentist?*

- *What positive experiences have you had with a dentist? What happened to make it a positive experience?*
- *What negative experiences have you had at the dentist? What happened to make it a negative experience?*
- *What can we do to make you more comfortable as a patient in our office?*

As you listen, pay attention to the patient's verbal and non-verbal communication. Do they seem nervous or ill at ease? Do they seem relaxed and confident? As the patient seems to open up, ask more probing questions, drilling down until you discover more about their basic emotional wants and needs. Questions like these can give you more details:

- *How do you feel about your teeth in general? How do you feel about your smile?*
- *If I could wave a magic wand, what would be your perfect smile?*
- *Are you ever reluctant to talk, smile, or laugh because you are unhappy or worried about the way your smile looks?*
- *How does the condition of your teeth affect what you can eat or drink? What changes have you had to make in your diet and routine because of your teeth?*

If your patient gives specific answers that indicate unhappiness with the current state of their mouth, such as a loose-fitting partial, gums that bleed, old or chipped fillings, crowns, or veneers, bad breath or unpleasant taste, or any other specific dental issue, address it specifically to get more information. Here are some examples:

- *Do you worry that your partial will come loose while you are eating or talking?*
- *Do your gums bleed when you brush your teeth? How about when you floss?*
- *Do you notice sensitivity to cold and/or sugar?*
- *Has anyone important to you ever told you that you have bad breath? How has that affected you? How does that make you feel?*
- *Has your doctor or pharmacist discussed the side effects (dry mouth) to the medication you are on?*
- *Has anyone ever explained to you how your diabetes and periodontal disease are linked together?*

Ask Questions to Determine Your Patient's Values

During your interview, ask questions designed to reveal what your patient values about their overall health, not just their teeth. As you discover those values, you will want to ask follow-up questions to help you learn the rules your patients use to demonstrate support for those values. It's important to realize that people not only have their own individual set of values, the rules they set up to support their values are as unique as they are, and may not be the same as yours. Let's look at example questions and follow-ups to demonstrate:

Question: What is the most important thing we can do for you today?

Answer: Make me feel relaxed and comfortable during the exam. **(Value)**

Follow-up: What does feeling relaxed and comfortable during the exam mean to you?

Answer: That I'm not in pain, I'm not too cold, my mouth isn't always full of water or saliva. **(Rules)**

Or...

Question: John, what is most important to you in your relationship with a dentist?

Answer: That the dentist respects me and my time. **(Value)**

Follow-up: What would have to happen for you to know that the dentist respects you and your time?

Answer: Being on time. Not talking down to me. Being a good listener. Allowing me to participate in making the final decision **(Rules)**

Or...

Question: What did you like most about your last dentist?

Answer: The dentist took the time to make sure I understood what he was doing. **(Value)**

Follow-up: What did he do, specifically, to make sure you understood?

Answer: He described what he was doing in words I could understand; he showed me pictures and videos about the procedure; he showed me with a mirror after each step. **(Rules)**

What is an important value to one patient may not be to another. And rules that demonstrate a value to one person may not to another. Using follow-up questions will help you truly get to know and understand your patients as individuals and provide them the quality of service and care that **they want**. (Remember: It's not about you. It's about them!)

Listen for Clues about Your Patient's Motivators and Buying Strategy

In the last chapter, we illustrated that pleasure and pain motivate people to take action. Combine that with the fact that each of us has our own general, pervasive, habitual communication pattern that reflects what we think, feel, and believe, both verbally and non-verbally. That means that each of us has a unique motivation or "buying strategy." Paying attention to the way your patient communicates will reveal his greatest motivator. Is it pleasure? Or is it pain?

When you are interviewing and presenting options to your patients, you want to understand what drives them to take action. You need to determine whether they are more motivated to seek the pleasure of something, or to avoid the pain of something. Are they directing their attention **toward** getting what they want (pleasure), or are they directing their attention **away** from something they don't want (pain).

In other words, people are motivated by **benefits** (moving toward) or **consequences** (moving away).

Let's ask a patient, "Mark, what is the most important thing to you about your smile?"

The patient replies, "I want to make sure I keep my natural teeth."

That indicates a motivating factor or "buying strategy" based on being drawn **toward** the **benefit**, toward getting what they want.

On the other hand, let's say the patient says, "I don't want to lose my natural teeth."

That response shows you the patient's motivating factor or "buying strategy" is to move **away** from and avoid the **consequences** of something he doesn't want.

Understanding what drives each individual patient – **toward or away, benefits or consequences** -- will help you tailor your approach to each individual patient. You'll get the same results, but you'll use a different communication strategy.

To test your understanding, consider the following statements, and determine whether they are designed to reveal **toward or away**, **pain or pleasure, benefit or consequences** as motivating factors or buying strategies:

The benefits to you of this treatment are ...

By accepting this treatment, you avoid ...

In order for you to get healthy, you want...

To avoid losing your teeth, you want...

As you are listening, you will want to pay attention not only to your patient's words, but also to their physical cues such as posture, facial expressions, gestures, and tonality (as we discussed in Chapter 5). Help your patient feel a sense of rapport with you, and help them like and trust you by mirroring, matching, and pacing.

Listen Carefully and Respond Directly Using Your Patient's Preferred Communication Modality

We discussed people's preferred communication modalities, those being visual, auditory, kinesthetic, and digital auditory. What will ensure your patient feels not only listened to, but also understood, is when you can respond to them what they are telling you, in their language. Here are some examples of responses for each communication modality:

Visual

- I see what you're saying...
- It looks like you've been unhappy about this for quite a while...
- What would your life look like if you felt your smile were exactly what you wanted?
- The picture I'm getting is that you'd like to have a brighter smile...
- So the light at the end of the tunnel for you would be to...

Auditory

- What I hear you saying is...
- Tell me more about that...
- So, is it fair to say that it's important for you to have this fixed?
- It sounds like this has been a problem for some time...
- Let me see if I've tuned in to what your saying...

Kinesthetic

- Describe the discomfort or pain...how long have you felt like this?

- What have you not been able to do because of this? What will you finally be able to do once we have fixed this?
- I feel like you're concerned about...
- What holds you back from...?
- How would it feel if you...?

Digital Auditory

- I understand you'd like...
- That makes sense to me...
- Would it be logical to assume...?
- I think we've figured out your main concern is...
- Help me understand your thinking process...

In designing your interview questions, be sure to include those that can reveal your patient's values, so that you can address them directly during the treatment planning conversation.

The patient interview is the first, most important step in effective treatment planning, which we will discuss in the next chapter. The more information you can get in your initial interview, the better able you will be to create a treatment plan that your patients will willingly accept.

Ideas for Action: Ask Questions that Give You the Important Information You Need

1. If your practice does not currently have a smile questionnaire or interview procedure in place, it's time to design one. Brainstorm with your team; even ask your loyal, long-term patients what you should include. Craft questions that help you get the kind of information that will help you interact more smoothly and professionally with your patients, and understand who they are, their preferred communication modality, what they value, what motivates them, and what they most deeply want. Contact us at **www.dmicoaching.com** if you would like assistance in this.

2. Create interview verbiage and practice using it with your treatment team. Take turns practicing listening and responding to different communication modalities. Take turns asking initial questions and follow-up questions so everyone understands how to reveal patient values, rules, and "buying strategies" or motivation factors.

3. Train your entire staff to listen more effectively and interact with each person as an individual.

Contact us at **www.dmicoaching.com** to assist you in this process.

In the next chapter, we'll build on the Patient Interview to develop a world-class handoff strategy that not only makes your patients feel well cared for, it might just make your job easier!

Chapter 8:

How to Present a Treatment Plan Your Patients Want

"Most dentists have a case acceptance rate of around 20% to 30%, which means that seven or eight out of 10 patients don't follow through with recommended treatment. When you and your team learn how to connect with patients on an emotional level, your case acceptance can increase to 60% and higher. Imagine doubling your revenue. [10]

"Let me think about it." "I have to talk to my husband/wife/partner." "My insurance won't pay for it." "But nothing hurts right now." "Let me check my work schedule." "I'm leaving town next month."

How many times have you heard responses like

---

[10] Kesner, Michael, D.D.S. (2012, August). Why Patients Say "I'll Think About It." *Dental Economics*. Retrieved from: http://www.dentaleconomics.com/08.2012

these after you and your team invested a half hour or more explaining your diagnosis and recommended treatment plan to your patient?

You're not alone. You're probably one of the dentists experiencing a less than stellar treatment acceptance rate. **You're hearing these responses seven or eight out of 10 times you present!** What would it do for you if you collected 2 million instead of 1 million? If you collected 4 million instead of 2 million? What could you do with that extra cash flow? If you want your acceptance rates to improve, you and your team are going to want to change the way you approach treatment planning.

Why do so many of your patients not accept treatment? Probably because you're telling them what they need instead of motivating them towards what they want.

Patients base their buying decisions on their emotions, and then justify the decision with logic.

People buy feelings, not things.

Let's demonstrate this principle.

Think about the last time you bought a car. Did you **need** the one you ended up buying or did you **want** it? You pictured yourself driving down the road with your favorite music blasting. The luxurious leather seats felt so good, and wow, that new car smell! You probably imagined how good you would feel showing it off to your friends, family, and colleagues, and how proud you would be about proving you could afford such a high-end make and model.

Emotional, right?

Sure, it might have been more **logical** to buy a late-model used car. A less prestigious make and model, with fewer luxury features, and for sure, a car with a lower sticker price, would have made much more sense.

But emotion will always trump logic.

When patients leave your office, you want them to be "**feeling**" about the treatment you propose, not "**thinking**" about it. That's going to require you and your team to work together and consistently connect with your patients emotionally, not just intellectually or logically.

There are five fundamentals required to design and present a treatment plan your patients will happily accept:

You and every member of your team must be committed to effective 5-Star treatment planning, from the person who answers your phone, to your treatment coordinator, your office manager, your clinical assistant, your hygienist, up to and including you, the dentist.

You and every member your team must **connect emotionally with your patients** – and **stay connected** --every step of the way, from their first telephone call right through to their after-care call.

You and every member of your team must **inspire and motivate** your patient to **want** the treatment they **need**.

You and every member of your team must **communicate the urgency** of making the decision to get treatment completed Now.

You and every member of your team must **reinforce your patient's buying decision** by focusing on the **benefits** of choosing treatment, and the **consequences** of not taking action now.

Let's explore each of these fundamentals.

Every Member of Your Team Must be Committed to Effective Treatment Planning

Your practice thrives or dies based on your financial success. When you can raise your treatment acceptance rate from 20-30% to 60-70%, everyone benefits: your patients, your team, your practice, you and your family.

You want to lead your team to understand the direct benefits and consequences, **to them**, of improved treatment acceptance rates. Their salaries, their benefits, and their bonuses all depend on a stable, steady income, and if the practice income increases, they will reap rewards in their paychecks, benefit's statements, and morale. Your team members have the ability to be their own CEO of their department for Your business and create their own economy utilizing these tools. With a proper, incentivizing bonus program based on individual departmental goals, your team will be eager to learn and cohesively work together towards your vision and goals.

Every Member of Your Team Must Connect Emotionally with Your Patients

In Chapter 5, we discussed ways to create rapport with anyone in 30 seconds or less, by realizing that more than 90% of the way people communicate is unconscious, and by recognizing that each person has a unique preferred communication modality. Those modalities are **Visual**, **Auditory**, **Kinesthetic**, and **Digital Auditory,** and reflect the ways people get, process and communicate information about the world through their five senses.

Creating rapport is the most important skill to master in order to improve communication with others, and the very foundation of persuasion and influence. The easiest, fastest way to create rapport with others happens when we recognize their preferred modality, and **mirror**, **match**, and **pace** that modality when interacting with them. **Match** and **mirror** their body language (posture, gestures, and facial expressions). **Pace** their speed, tone, and volume of speech. Use words that match their preferred language style.

Every team member must understand and use these

keys to creating rapport. **Train your team to note your patient's preferred communication style** so that **each team member can reference it** and interact more effectively with the patient on each and every visit. Also, make note of any amenities a patient requests so you have it ready and waiting for them before you bring them back to the operatory. Do they get cold easily and request a blanket? Do they like neck pillows? A warm lavender towel after their procedure? A hand-held mirror to check their make-up before you walk them to checkout?

Every Member of Your Team Must Inspire and Motivate Your Patient, to Want the Treatment They Need

In Chapter 6, we discussed the elements of persuasion and influence, and how they work together to shift our patients needs to wants.

What is the understanding of this word we use mistakenly so often in our diagnosis?

Need = Human requirement to provide for our survival, health and well-being.

If that is a simplistic description of the term "need", then what is our understanding of "want"?

Want = A personal desire to meet those needs.

Our needs give rise to wants and our wants are the pathway to meet our needs.

To inspire and motivate, requires mastery of persuasion and influence. Your new patient interview (Chapter 7) is essential to this process. You and your team ask questions and gather the information you need to discover your patient's underlying needs, values, rules, motivating factors, and buying strategies. You'll then build on that information during the Treatment Plan so you can assist your patient to make an emotionally satisfying decision they can then justify with logic.

Just as with your patient interview, the Treatment Plan conversation will require you to be keenly aware of the following:

Underlying wants (emotional needs)

The patient came to see you for a unique **emotional** reason. What is it? Are they in pain? Are they concerned about their smile? Are they worried about old/failing previous dental work? Are they concerned about their physical attractiveness? Are they embarrassed about their appearance? Are they afraid of the potential pain of the treatment? Are they in financial distress, worried about the cost of treatment?

The place to start with any conversation about proposed treatment is right there: in the patient's expressed (or discovered) emotional state. Acknowledge their emotional state, using their words if possible:

"Charles, I can't imagine how you have been managing the pain and sensitivity that your cracked tooth must be causing you. Won't it be wonderful when it you can eat and drink without pain?"

"Jake, you mentioned your new sales job has you meeting clients and you have been concerned that your two front teeth have shifted and turned to the point that people are noticing it now. Imagine how confident you will feel when we create your new beautiful smile!"

"Hana, I know you are concerned about the investment to place a crown on your back tooth. You quite possibly are one bite away from your tooth breaking completely which could lead to a root canal, extraction and an implant. That would mean more time, more

appointments and more cost than simply doing a crown now and saving the tooth."

Values and the Rules that Support Them

Discovering your patient's values and the underlying rules that support them can help you present treatment solutions in a language they understand emotionally. Again, acknowledge them directly, using the patient's own words if possible:

"Kasey, you said what you trusted about your last dentist was his honesty and willingness to let you be a part of your treatment planning. Let me explain what we found during the exam, and show you a couple of options for treatment."

"Lauren, you said what's important to you is fixing your bite without breaking your budget. Here are two ways we can get that done for you, and you can choose the option that fits your lifestyle best."

"Kristen, you said your primary concern is that we respect your need to take time off work for treatment. Here's a schedule that will take care of the problem in just two one-hour visits over the next two weeks."

Buying Strategies

"Toward" versus "Away"

As a recap, people are motivated or driven by two states: pleasure or pain. They usually move **toward** pleasure, and **away** from pain. Of the two, **the avoidance of pain is usually a much stronger emotion than seeking pleasure**. (Just ask anyone who's ever complained of being overweight: while being overweight is painful, it's far less painful to sit around and eat donuts than it is to put the remote down, get off the couch, and go to the gym!)

It may seem painful to take action (anticipated pain of the treatment or financial pain due to the cost of treatment), but until the pain of not taking action is greater, your patient will likely stay with the familiar.

If you ask a patient, for example, *"Michelle, what is most important to you about your teeth?"* the patient's response will indicate to you which buying strategy is likely the strongest:

If your patient says, *"I want to keep my natural teeth,"* it indicates she is more likely to move **toward** the **benefits** of treatment.

On the other hand, if your patient says, *"I don't want to lose my teeth,"* you can see she is more likely to be motivated **away from the consequences** of avoiding treatment.

In your treatment conversation, you can experiment with toward and away language to see which is a more powerful buying strategy for your patient:

"The benefits to you of this treatment are ..."

"By accepting this treatment you avoid ..."

"In order for you to get healthy, you want (Protocol)."

"To avoid losing your teeth, you want (Protocol)."

"Big Picture" versus "Details"

Ask your patient directly whether they want to hear a broad overview of your treatment strategy, or a detailed explanation of what's involved. Then be certain you respect their preference, reassuring them that if they'd like more detail, you can provide it.

If you give a lot of detail to a person who prefers just the big picture, they will become anxious and distracted. Their eyes will glaze over, and more than likely, they will not accept treatment. If you give too broad a picture to a detail person, they are likely to feel dismissed or disrespected, and again, unlikely to accept your diagnosis.

Big Picture: *"The treatment I recommend involves three crowns and two fillings. It will take two visits and we can get it done in three weeks. You said earlier, you are leaving town next month and if it were me Donna, I would want to get those done right away because (Emotional Motivator)".*

Details: *"I highly recommend a crown on #7 because... First, we'll remove the cracked and decayed tooth structure, then... You said earlier, you are leaving town next month and if it were me Donna, I would want to get those done right away because (Emotional Motivator)".*

"Possibility" versus "Necessity"

Some people are more risk-tolerant, more likely to be motivated **toward** staying healthy, and will accept treatment based on that **possibility**. On the other hand, some patients, especially emergency patients, will only accept treatment that is necessary, with little interest in continuing care or complex treatment plans.

For example, offering a bonus like "Free whitening for a healthy mouth" might appeal to a "possibility patient," but be of little interest to a "necessity patient."

Every Member of Your Team Must Communicate the Urgency of Deciding in Favor of Treatment

Even the most skilled treatment coordinator or dentist will encounter resistance when presenting a treatment plan to their patients. Patients will object to the cost, complain about the required time or inconvenience, or express concern about the nature of the treatment. It's human nature, and it's not personal.

In any sales situation, including Treatment Planning, there are always two sales happening at the same time: you and your team are selling a treatment plan to your patient, and at the same time, your patient is selling you their limiting beliefs of why they cannot do treatment now. Your goal is to help guide and influence your patients to say, "Yes" to the treatment they need and deserve.

This process calls for your powers of influence, through a six-step process:

Establish Rapport

Before you can persuade or influence anyone, you

must have that close connection. We've discussed rapport at length, focusing on communication styles, mirroring, matching, pacing, and identifying with our patients' experiences and model of the world. Make it your overriding mission to establish rapport with everyone who walks in your door, and you and your team will become more successful.

Ask Questions

Beginning with the first phone call, through the New Patient Interview, and included as part of the Treatment Plan, use questions to discover their emotional motivators (their innermost needs and values) and their buying strategy. Your goal in getting them to "yes" is to align what you learn, with their treatment plan.

Questions like the following will help you discover your patient's emotional motivators:

"Michael, wouldn't you like/love to have...?"

"Katie, you can...can't you?"

"Brooke, isn't it time to...?"

"Bodhi, aren't you tired of (the same old thing)...?"

"Shea, can you imagine...?"

"Megan, do you ever ask yourself...?"

"Jodie, have you ever wondered what it might look like to...?"

Acknowledge and Confirm What Your Patient Shares With You

Acknowledge and confirm your patient's answers to these exploratory questions, using their words verbatim, with the same modality, mirroring and pacing their tone, pitch, inflection, speed, and volume. Listen for key words and repeat them.

"Shawn, so you would love to have... (Their words verbatim). Is that how you're feeling?"

"Linda, you are saying it's time to... (Their words, verbatim). Am I hearing you correctly?"

"Tim, you are imagining... (Their words verbatim). Have I got the picture?"

Connect Need with Consequence, Emotional Motivator, then Solution

Explain the consequences of doing nothing then follow up with connecting what they want, with why they want it, to your solution.

Close

In the most successful practices, the doctor and hygienist only hand the patient over to the treatment coordinator when they have overcome all their patient's objections.

Closing is simply a matter of assuming the patient is accepting treatment and guiding them to schedule.

You will know immediately if you haven't sufficiently addressed their objections or created enough value when they say:

"Let me think about it."

"I have to check my schedule."

"Wow, I can't possibly afford that."

Use those statements as opportunities to ask more questions, dig a little deeper, and explore the deep want/emotional need that's preventing them from saying "yes." Why is this so important? Because they are placing more value on not accepting treatment than they are on getting healthy.

Overcome any Objections

It may seem counterintuitive, but the best way to overcome a patient objection is to acknowledge it and agree with it.

To acknowledge another's words is to accept them at face value, with nothing added. It's a sign of respect. It indicates you've heard and understand them, and builds on the trust you've created throughout the process so far. The more the patient trusts you and feels understood, the more easily you can reach agreement with them.

Acknowledgment is nothing more than repeating their own words, with their own inflection and emphasis, and empathizing with the emotion that may be attached.

"Chad, you feel the price is beyond your budget."

"Arika, you're shocked at how expensive this is."

"Sheryl you're worried about the time this will take you away from work."

The next part of overcoming the objection is to agree with them.

What's that we're saying? Agree with them?

Yes, absolutely. Agree with them. Here's why.

In their world, dental treatment IS expensive. In their world, time away from their workplace IS inconvenient. In their world, a financial decision like this WILL require a conversation with their spouse. In their world, they are right! Acknowledge, Agree and reframe their responses.

"Joan. Investing in a crown is expensive and it will get even more expensive when your tooth breaks."

Once you've acknowledged and agreed with their point of view, ask more questions for clarification.

"Jeannie, what if you did have money to invest in this treatment, where would it come from?"

"John, what is holding you back from scheduling today?"

"Jack, what monthly investment would you be able to afford, if we were able to work out a financing option?"

It's your duty and obligation to provide the service and treatment your patient needs. You might have to make them uncomfortable enough with their status quo, that the only relief will be to take the leap and accept treatment. Said another way, **they know they "need it," you have to make them "want it."**

Use questions that disturb the patient's reality enough to get them to think outside the box and see the possibilities, and guide the patient to solve his or her own problems. Your questions, based on your sincere desire to see the patient get healthy, are the secrets to getting the patient to "yes."

Every Member of Your Team Must Reinforce Your Patient's Buying Decision

To transform your practice, dramatically increase your treatment acceptance rate, and create a roster of loyal, happy patients who rave about you and your team, everyone on the team must reinforce the core message: this is a patient-centered practice, focused on meeting patients' needs. Every team member must be clear about the benefits of treatment and the consequences of avoiding treatment, and reinforce that message during every step of the patient's process.

That means your front desk or scheduling coordinator reinforces the benefit of keeping appointments, arriving on time (or early) and providing complete information. Your hygienist and assistant reinforce the benefits of follow-up treatment and following instructions or protocols.

You reinforce the benefits of moving to the next step in the treatment plan. The treatment or financial coordinator reinforces the benefit of scheduling treatment and creating a financial arrangement that works for everyone.

When everyone is on the same team, playing by the same rules, treatment planning becomes much less stressful, much more productive, and much more profitable. It is your win – win.

Ideas for Action: Design a Treatment Plan Procedure for Your Practice

1. Brainstorm with your office manager, treatment coordinator and patient coordinator all of the reasons patients give for declining treatment. In our experience, you'll find those reasons falling into four main categories: fear of money, time, inconvenience, and pain.

2. For each main objection, brainstorm with your team all of the possible questions you might ask a patient to help them solve their money, time, inconvenience, and pain concerns.

3. From these brainstorming sessions, set aside time to practice role-playing with one another. Pay particular attention to role-playing scenarios you find most challenging to overcome.

Contact us at www.dmicoaching.com to assist you in this process.

Chapter 9: How to Practice a Perfect Patient Hand-Off

> *"The hand-off is literally handing the patient from one team member to the next. This means never leaving a patient alone without letting them know who and what to expect next. It means never dropping them off at the front desk to a team member on the phone, or abandoning them in a treatment room wondering how long they'll be there and who they will see next. It means preparing your patient every step of the way by explaining who and what comes next, anticipating their needs and expectations, and introducing them to the next team member, thereby setting them up for a successful appointment."*[11]

When was the last time you overheard a patient raving with pleasure about the precision of your drilling, your mastery of the intricacies of replacing old amalgams, or the sheer beauty of the impression you took for their new crown?

[11] Hagerman, J., RDH, BSDH. Perfecting the Hand-Off. (2012, October). ***Dental Economics***. Retrieved from: http://www.dentaleconomics.com

You haven't, because they don't.

Your patients don't care about the technicalities of your job. Most of them assume that if you have a "Dentist" sign in your office window, the place is clean, and their friend recommended you, you're qualified to provide adequate dental treatment. Sure, clinical skill and professional competence are important, but to your patients, there's something much more important:

How do you treat them as human beings? Does their experience in your office verify that you know them and care about them? Is there a seamless process in place that transfers them from one team member to the next? Do they experience the same level of care and concern each step of the way?

Does the hygienist or clinical assistant just hand the patient's file to the dentist without a word? Does the treatment coordinator walk the patient to the front desk and plop their file on the counter with a simple thanks and goodbye?

You and your team must function like an Olympic relay team, with each member clearly focused on passing the patient successfully and smoothly to the next team member.

Why is the hand-off so important?

The patient hand-off is quite literally a transfer of power. When one team member takes the time to get to know and understand who the patient is, what the patient wants, and what the patient needs, they have the power in the patient's eyes. The team member then transfers that power to the next team member in line with an introduction of the patient, an explanation of what is important to the patient, what was done and what will happen next, reaffirming to the patient that the next team member is an expert in what they do.

Designing and implementing a clear, consistent hand-off involves everyone on your team, and is vital to the success of your practice. Such a protocol...

- ✓ **Explains** what you propose to do, what you have done, and what you will do next so your patient is clear about the process
- ✓ **Demonstrates your commitment to the patient** by conveying what they have shared with you using their own key words
- ✓ **Reassures your patients** they have come to the right place at the right time
- ✓ **Reinforces the doctor's recommendations**
- ✓ **Educates the patient and helps him or her understand** the proposed treatment, leaving little

room for misunderstanding or surprises

- ✓ **Confirms the sense of urgency** necessary to schedule and complete the recommended treatment

- ✓ **Sets you up for a comfortable treatment presentation,** and **Increases your treatment acceptance rate** and scheduling success

- ✓ Results in **happier patients who are more likely to recommend your practice** enthusiastically to their friends, family and colleagues

- ✓ Helps you **run your practice more efficiently**

- ✓ Provides a **win – win for the patient, your team and your practice**

Who is involved in the hand-off?

Every member of your team, both administrative and clinical, is necessary to an optimal patient experience. Therefore, each team member must be involved in, and committed to, a smooth, efficient hand-off.

Again, think of it as a relay. Every contact between any member of your team and your patient is involved in this relay, and "dropping the baton" at any step during the process can damage the relationship of trust you and your team are trying to build.

Therefore, every team member needs training in your hand-off process.

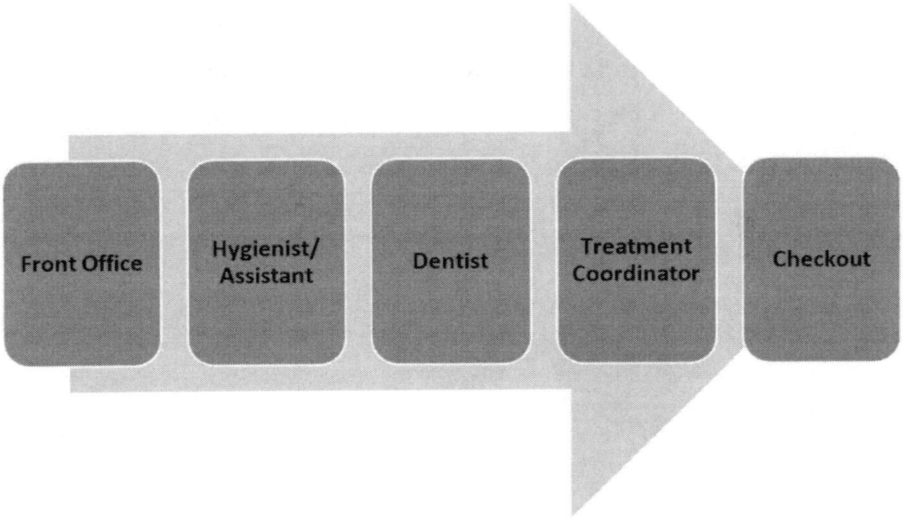

What skills are required for a perfect hand-off process?

The perfect hand-off relies on effective communication skills, both in listening and speaking and, unfortunately, it cannot rely on a predictable script. Each hand-off will be different, depending on the patient and the level of rapport you have established.

Listen carefully.

The first step in developing that rapport, and the highest honor you can give your patients, is to **listen carefully**, without interruption. Slow down. Observe their preferred communication style. Repeat, what you are hearing, using their words, to let them know you have heard and understood them. Take notes and ask questions to ensure you are hearing their words, emotions, and concerns accurately.

Take the time to tune in to your patients, finding out who they are as people. Get to know them, and show interest in their personal concerns. Ask about birthdays, anniversaries, vacations, reunions, weddings, pregnancies, or other special occasions that might be enhanced by a great dental experience. Your patient may not necessarily volunteer their story, so it's up to you to discover what it is. Ask questions like the following to every new patient.

- *Tell me about some of the dental treatment you have had in the past.* As they tell you, ask them to tell you a little more about that. *Why did you have that done?*

- *How long has it been since you have had any dental work? What has kept you away for so long?*
- *Do you have any missing teeth? Has anyone ever suggested anything about replacing them?*
- *Are you worried about any stains or spots on your teeth?*
- *Is there anything else about your teeth that concerns you?*
- *How would you rate the appearance of your teeth on a scale of 1-10? Why a seven? What would make it a 10?*
- *Why did you leave your last dentist? What did you like most about your last dentist? What did you like least about your last dentist?*
- *"I know Jane, this is a lot of questions and we want to make sure we give you just what you want and just what you need."*

Acknowledge what your patient is telling you.

As you listen, **acknowledge** what they are telling you. Words of acknowledgement include

I hear you saying...

So what you are telling me is...

It seems like your biggest concern is...

Let me see if I understand you...

It sounds like you feel...

Acknowledgement does not necessarily mean you agree with what your patient is saying. All it means is that you have heard and understood them.

Empathize with their concerns.

Acknowledgement also gives you permission to feel what the world might feel like from their model of the world and **express your empathy**.

> Your patient says, "*Every single time I've been to the dentist, it has been horribly painful. I just know this one will be, too.*"
>
> You simply **acknowledge and empathize with their belief**: *"Wow, Jordan, it sounds like you have had some painful experiences with dentists in the past. The good news is you have shared your concerns with us so we can provide you with what it is you want and need."*

Reassure the patient you can address their concerns. Asking questions, listening to your patients, and acknowledging and empathizing with their experiences gives you a powerful opportunity to **reassure your patients** they've come to the right place!

Speak simple English, not just "Dentist."

Every profession has its own language, or jargon. While you may speak "dentist" fluently, chances are your patient doesn't understand your acronyms, buzzwords, or verbal shortcuts. Carefully observe your patient's facial expressions as you explain things to them or hand them off to the next team member. Since you're handing off verbally, in front of the patient, it's important they understand what you're saying about them and their treatment. *Remember, when someone is talking about us, we listen to every word they say.

Repeat. Repeat. Repeat.

As you hand off the patient to your next team member, you will pass along the information you have gathered, out loud, so the patient hears it. Why? **It takes the average patient at least five repetitions before they can fully hear, digest, and understand** the treatment you are proposing and your reasons for proposing it. This reinforcement, from team member to team member, using the same verbiage, leads the patient to an obvious conclusion: this team understands me, they see what I want, they hear what my concerns are and they care about how I feel.

Also, when people talk at us, we tend to zone out. When people talk about us to someone else, **we hear every word they say........**

Practice to create Excellence!

Handing off the patient effectively from one team member to another might make logical sense, and until each member of the team is trained and managed to repeat, repeat, repeat, only then will it become a habit. Make a point of reinforcing a great hand-off every time you experience it. Provide feedback to your team when they don't hand off effectively, and guide them to recognize what they missed. A high-performing team does not happen by accident, and neither does a perfect hand-off. It's like the old New York joke: "How do you get to Carnegie Hall? Practice. Practice. Practice.

What does the perfect hand-off look like?

While it is next to impossible to write a rigid script for the perfect handoff, you and your team must realize that patient hand-offs start the moment your patient calls to schedule an appointment, and occurs throughout every step of their process with you, even during your post treatment care call.

Whether your patient is an anxious teenager, an overworked sales person, or a high-powered executive, every patient who walks into your practice wants to know:

- *"Where are you taking me?*
- *Who will I be seeing?*
- *What will they be doing to me?*
- *How long will it take?*
- *Will it hurt?*
- *How much will it cost?*
- *When can I get out of here?"*[12]

So the perfect hand-off starts by understanding those basic patient concerns, and answering those questions before the patient even asks them. As we said at the beginning of this Chapter, you and your team must

---

[12] Ibid

function like an Olympic relay team, with each member clearly focused on passing the patient, like a torch, smoothly to the next team member.

Essentially, the hand-off is a 5-step process:

1. Greet the patient by name. Explain your role in the process.

2. Gather information about the patient's concerns (wants, needs) and general medical issues. Verify your understanding of the patient's concerns and issues with acknowledgment, empathy, and reassurance.

3. Explain what you are going to do and why, and tell them how much time is involved.

4. Explain what you have done, and tell the patient what will happen next, who they will see, and why.

5. Introduce them to your expert team member by name. Summarize what has been done; summarize the patient concerns (wants, needs) and issues. Reassure the patient that the next expert team member is going to take great care of them.

Every member of the dental team wants to be ready, focused, and listening carefully, to receive the patient hand-off, so that they can fully understand who the patient is and what the patient needs. And each team member must be responsible for making sure they have received all the information they need to provide an optimal, 5 - Star patient experience.

The following chart is a simple illustration of each step of the hand-off.

Front Office To Back Office

- Greet the patient by name within 5 seconds of walking in
- Gathers information, complete any necessary paperwork
- Introduces the patient to the hygienist/clinical assistant
- Explains the patients concerns and known personal motivator
- Clinician greets the patient, shakes their hand, builds rapport

Hygienist/ Clinical Assistant To Doctor

- Hygienist/Assistant introduces Doctor to patient
- Doctor greets the patient, shakes their hand, builds rapport
- Hygienist/Assistant explains patient's concerns and personal motivator
- Hygienist/Assistant explains treatment completed and areas of concern

Doctor To Hygienist/Assistant

- Doctor affirms findings to Hygienist/Assistant
- Doctor acknowledges patient concerns and personal motivators
- Doctor explains what was completed, what will happen next and answers patient's questions
- Doctor thanks patient and hands patient back to Hygienist/Assistant

Clinician To Treatment Coordinator

- Clinician introduces patient to Treatment Coordinator and explains what was completed and what will happen next
- Explains patient concerns and personal motivators then thanks patient
- Treatment Coordinator offers financial options
- Introduces patient to checkout, explains patient concerns, describes next steps (If they did not check patient out)

Treatment Coordinator To Checkout

- Treatment Coordinator introduces patient to checkout and explains what has been completed, next steps, patient's concerns and personal motivators
- Checkout greets patient and acknowledges steps above
- Completes next steps, answers questions and collect payment
- Thanks patient for their business

It is, important for you and your team to work out the language and approach that best suits your practice and area of specialty.

Here are some examples of efficient hand-offs to get you started:

> **<u>Front Office to Clinical Team</u>:** *Janie, this is Megan and she is visiting our office for the first time. John Smith is a good friend of hers and he referred her to our office. Megan is getting married in June, so she is really excited and wants to have Doctor take a look at a couple of her front teeth and learn a little more about teeth whitening. She also has a bit of sensitivity in her lower gums*
>
> *Megan, Janie is a fantastic hygienist and she will take care of you today. Have a great visit!*

> **<u>Clinical team to Doctor:</u>** *Doctor Maxwell, this is Megan. Megan is visiting us for the first time. She works with John Smith at the Community College. He recommended she come and see you before her wedding in June. She really wants to fix her front, bottom teeth and get some teeth whitening before her wedding parties start. We have done a full set of x-rays and pictures. She is experiencing some gum sensitivity, she had 5 bleeding points and 2 "4's" during probing, and I showed her the pictures of her cracked tooth. Megan and I have discussed what could happen with her cracked tooth if she doesn't take care of it now, and the possibility of needing a root canal and crown. Megan is also taking medication, and has a history of*

diabetes. I explained to Megan how diabetes affects her gingivitis, and I have recommended she purchase ...

Megan, this is Dr. Maxwell. He is going to take great care of you and make sure your smile is beautiful for your wedding.

Doctor to Patient: (Sit down facing your patient, look patient in the eyes, smile, maintain a confident posture, mirror your patients tonality and physiology). *Hi Megan, I am Dr. Maxwell. It is great to meet you (shake hands). So, John Smith recommended you come see me. We really like him. Kristen tells me you are getting married in June! That is exciting! Well, let's get you taken care of so you have the smile you want for your wedding. Tell me about the sensitivity you are feeling.*

(Do exam, review x-rays/pictures) *Megan, Janie is correct, you have a crack in your lower left tooth (show picture) and a crack ignored turns into a broken tooth causing possible root canal, extraction, and an implant. In my experience, these things happen at the worst times, like when you are trying to enjoy your wedding parties!*

Let's keep this simple and protect you and your tooth with a crown to maintain its structure because you don't want to be dealing with pain and all those appointments from a broken tooth around your wedding, do you (command lower tone)? *I agree. Megan, I want you to get on my schedule immediately so we can take care of you before your tooth breaks, and complete your whitening so you're teeth will look perfect in your wedding pictures. Megan, do you prefer mornings or afternoons? Janie, what morning appointments do we have available this week?*

Hygienist to Treatment Coordinator: *Taylor, this is Megan and she has a big day coming up in June! She is getting married and we are going to do a crown and teeth whitening so she will have a beautiful smile. We have discussed Megan's cracked tooth and its effect on her mouth and her overall health, especially since she has a history of diabetes. We have prioritized her treatment for you. Megan knows she needs to start taking action now so she can look great and feel great in time for her special day. We have already scheduled her appointments, she is concerned about finances, and I told her you would assist her in fitting the treatment into her lifestyle.*

Megan, it was great meeting you. You did a fantastic job today. Taylor is our expert in financing and she is going to make this work for you! See you in a few days!

If each member of your team commits to handle each patient in a positive, affirming way, your patient will feel cared for in every interaction, as if each team member is an active advocate for your patient's health and well-being.

When your patients experience that level of care, they are more inspired to become loyal, raving fans of your practice, and more importantly, a steady source of referrals and new production for your practice.

Ideas for Action: Create Your Perfect Hand-Off Process

1. Evaluate your current hand-off procedure with your team, on a scale of 1-10, with 1 being non-existent and 10 being stellar.

2. Brainstorm with your team the areas you could improve so that every team member feels supported in handing off your patients effectively to the next team member.

3. If you do not currently have a hand-off protocol in your office, **Contact us** at **info@dmicoaching.com** for assistance in designing an impactful and successful hand off.

Chapter 10: Setting Up Your Systems for Success

When was the last time you experienced frustration at the office? What caused it? Was it because somebody on your team didn't follow up or follow through or just plain forgot to do something? Was it because you assumed they would know what to do and when to do it?

If you're like most doctors who manage teams, chances are you were disappointed as well as frustrated. Perhaps you took it personally. And it's perfectly human (although not particularly healthy) to take that frustration out on other people. That's why so many doctors find managing others so challenging.

What if, instead of looking at the source of your frustration as a personal failure or "personnel problem," you could evaluate it differently?

It's been our experience that most of the frustration, disappointment, drama, and chaos among team members originates from misunderstanding or miscommunication. What allows for misunderstanding and miscommunication? **Lack of clear, specific systems that everyone knows, understands, and agrees to follow.**

In other words, what if it wasn't a personal failure at all? What if it was a **system** failure?

If you experience an above-average level of frustration, disappointment, drama, or even chaos in your practice, look for solutions in your systems.

As the leader of a successful dental practice, you must **manage systems**, and **lead people**.

What is a "System?"

System:

1. A set of **detailed methods, procedures, and routines** created to carry out a **specific activity, perform a duty, or solve a problem**.
2. An **organized, purposeful structure** that consists of interrelated and interdependent elements (components, entities, factors, members, parts etc.). These **elements continually influence one another** (directly or indirectly) to maintain their activity and the existence of the system, in order to achieve the goal of the system.

All systems have **(a) inputs, outputs and feedback mechanisms**, (b) **maintain an internal steady-state** (called homeostasis) despite a changing external environment, **(c) display properties that are different than the whole** (called emergent properties) but are not possessed by any of the individual elements, and (d) **have boundaries that are usually defined by the system observer.**[13]

---

[13] System. BusinessDictionary.com. Retrieved June 17, 2017, from BusinessDictionary.com: http://www.businessdictionary.com/definition/system.html.

In your dental practice, **detailing and documenting your methods, procedures, and routines**, creating an office training and protocols manual, then **leading your team to manage and follow them**, will not only ease frustration, it provides a wealth of benefits to your practice.

Why focus on systems?

There are many tangible benefits to your practice in defining and managing systems. Here are just a few important reasons you and your team will want to focus on systems:

- Clearly established systems **make your practice more efficient** by ensuring consistency and accuracy of your procedures, processes, routines, and policies.

- Documented systems and procedures help you **correct or eliminate mistakes, avoid duplication of effort, and clear up confusion.**

- Analyzing and setting up systematic ways of doing business will help you **reduce costs**.

- Well-documented systems allow you to **train, motivate, and supervise your team more effectively,** and provide a structure to **help new team members get up to speed** quickly.

- When you clearly define your systems, **team members become more accountable** for their own job success, and can "own" their own results.

- When team members are empowered by clearly defined systems, their **morale improves, there are fewer misunderstandings, disagreements, or frustrations** with each other**,** they **work smarter together** and they are much happier, creating a culture of success.

- "Systemizing" your business **allows you to lead the people and manage the practice**.

- Setting up and managing effective systems can help you see a dramatic **improvement in your income**, often very quickly.

- Once your systems are in place and running efficiently, you can now **free up time** to **enjoy doing what you love to do.**

Where to Start: First Things First.

1. What is the state of your practice right now?

Are you making the kind of money you'd like? Do you have a growing, thriving patient base? Do you have a happy, motivated team that looks forward to coming in to work every day?

Look at everything through the eyes of a patient. Start at the front door; walk through your reception area, into the treatment room, consultation room, even the restroom. What's working? What's not working? Make a list. It might be a long one.

Do you have effective systems in place? Have you documented your systems in writing? How well are they working? Does your entire team understand and follow them? Where are there breakdowns or inefficiencies?

Once you've taken a clear-eyed look at the truth of where your practice stands, it's time to start. Here is where your team can help.

2. Know your numbers.

Management guru Peter Drucker is often quoted as saying, "What gets measured gets managed." To restate him, we say, "**If you don't measure it, you can't possibly manage it**."

The definition of "systems" that we began this chapter with tells us that all systems have inputs, outputs, and **feedback mechanisms**. Measuring and tracking your numbers provides you feedback about how well your system is working.

What should you measure? In a word, everything. There are over 25 systems in your practice that need to be managed.

Measure everything related to time and money, from how many rings before your front office answers the phone, to how many referrals you're getting from each patient, to the dollar amount each patient represents to your practice. Although it's harder to measure, consider tracking intangibles like job satisfaction, morale, and patient satisfaction. Here's just a **partial list** of what you'll want to track and measure.

- **Time**
    - Average number of rings before picking up a call
    - Average waiting time to book an appointment
    - Average waiting time on the phone, in reception, in the chair
    - Processing time at the lab
    - Supply or equipment delivery time
    - Hygiene appointments staying on time
    - Doctor's appointments staying on time
- **Money**
    - Revenue (daily, weekly, monthly, quarterly, annually)
    - Hourly productivity
    - Average dollar value of each patient
    - Account Receivables

    - Fixed costs (rent, utilities, equipment, leases, insurance, taxes, etc.)
    - Human Resources costs (salaries, benefits, bonuses, training, insurance, etc.)
    - Costs of supplies, labs
    - Profit margins
    - Return on investment (ROI) from marketing campaigns
- **Intangibles**
    - Patient satisfaction
    - Employee satisfaction/morale/culture
    - Personal job satisfaction

*For a more detailed list, contact DMI Coaching.

As you remember, if you don't measure it, you can't possibly manage it. And if you can't measure and manage it, how can you improve it?

3. **Set goals, set up systems, and track your progress.**

Once you've measured where you are, you can **set specific, measurable goals** for yourself, your practice, and your team.

And once you've set goals based on your measurements, guess what? You're going to want to **set up systems and track your progress toward your goals**.

Let's say, for example, that you calculate your average income per patient (annual practice revenue ÷ number of patients you see per year) is $1500. If your goal is to increase overall practice revenue, you'll want to include raising the average income per patient from $1500 to $2000. So you set that as a goal:

Goal: In this fiscal year, we will raise our average income per patient by $500.

Then you'll set up a system to track it. Your system could be as simple as a chart on a white board in the back office or a spreadsheet on the computer that tracks numbers by the day, week, month, quarter, and year.

Here's another example, a simple goal. You find, after observing for a week, that your patients, on average, sit in reception for 10-15 minutes beyond their scheduled appointment time.

Goal: Patients will be seated in the treatment room within 5 minutes of their appointment time.

System: Front and back team members communicating immediately when patient is ready via scheduler and inter-office communication systems. Front office team tracks the time, in the scheduler, of when the patient is actually brought back for treatment. If patient has waited more than 15 minutes, a goody bag is presented with an apology and noted in the patients account.

Tracking: Front office will log all patients brought back more than 5 minutes late and discuss in the next morning huddle. Office manager will evaluate team members continually running late and appointments not scheduled properly.

Here's a third example, just for emphasis. Let's say you've discovered you are only getting ten new patients each month. You'd like to improve those numbers by getting more referrals from existing patients. So many practices have forgotten the power of internal marketing. Get your entire team on-board and inspired to ask every patient for a referral.

Goal: 20 new patients each month.

System: Set up a patient referral rewards program along with a system to track them. Offer existing patients an incentive to refer their family and friends. Create a contest for your team to hand out their business cards to people in their community. Send an email blast, or offer a care to share card at checkout and communicate the rewards program to your existing patients.

Tracking: Ask every new patient, when they call, how they heard about your practice and record the referral source. Have one team member responsible for sending out welcome and thank you cards to each new patient and referral source. Weekly, run your new patient list and verify every patient has a referral source. Have monthly or quarterly contests for your patients to win a gift for referring the most new patients. Market and advertise this on all your social media sites.

Setting goals and tracking results is the only way to confirm movement. If you want your team's performance to improve, you must find ways to measure their performance, set goals, and track the results. If you want to create a thriving, bustling practice and a healthy, increasing income, you must find ways to measure where you are, set goals, and track your results. If you do not have trackers in place, we can help you with this. We have coached practices on the refinement of their systems as well as implemented systems, front to back, in new practice start-ups.

4. **Create an Operations Manual for your practice.** Your Operations Manual is perhaps the most critical key to making sure your team understands how your practice works and functions. It's the playbook for your team, the central collection point for every one of your systems, policies, and procedures. If a key team member suddenly quits, the person replacing them should be able to turn to your Operations Manual and find exactly what they need in order to do the job.

You can set up your own structure, but make sure your Operations Manual includes:

- **Job descriptions and key performance indicators (KPIs) for each position on your team.**

  Job descriptions typically include[14]:

  - Job title
  - Job objective or overall purpose statement

[14] Small Business Administration. *Writing Effective Job Descriptions*. U.S. Government. Retrieved 06/17/2017 from: https://www.sba.gov/starting-business/hire-retain-employees/writing-effective-job-descriptions

- Summary of the general nature and level of the job
- Description of the broad function and scope of the position
- List of duties or tasks performed critical to success
- Checklist of daily, weekly and monthly task completion
- Key functional and relational responsibilities in order of significance
- Description of the relationships and roles within the company, including supervisory positions, subordinating roles and other working relationships

Key Performance Indicators (KPIs) are the key numbers to manage your employee's performance in the critical parts of their job. KPIs show the progress (or lack of it) toward realizing your practice objectives or strategic plans by monitoring the activities which (if not properly performed) would likely cause severe losses or outright failure.[15]

- **Standard Operating Procedures (SOPs) and checklists for every task**

A Standard Operating Procedure (SOP) is a written procedure that defines repetitive tasks according to agreed upon specifications, aimed

[15] key performance indicator (KPI). BusinessDictionary.com. Retrieved June 17, 2017, from BusinessDictionary.com: http://www.businessdictionary.com/definition/key-performance-indicator-KPI.html.

at obtaining a desired outcome. [16]A checklist is the "informal cousin" of an SOP. For example, you might want to include SOPs for setting appointments, conducting new patient interviews, filing patient records, cleaning the treatment area, ordering supplies, opening the office every morning, shutting down at night, and so forth. Your SOPs and checklists need to be clear, specific, and so clearly written that virtually anybody could follow the instructions.

- **Policies**

  Policies are the "governing principles," if you will, of your practice. They determine how you will behave, what can be expected of you and your practice, in specific circumstances. Detail, in writing, every policy that directs your practice. What are your policies, for example, on patient referrals? Complaints or requests for refunds? Flexible payment plans?

  In addition to your policies regarding your patients and how you conduct business with them, you'll want to include all of your human resources policies: vacation planning, sick leave, overtime, flextime, and so forth. Don't forget to clearly state your policies regarding online behavior, and how your team's use of social media could affect your practice.

---

[16] standard operating procedure (SOP): BusinessDictionary.com. Retrieved June 17, 2017, from BusinessDictionary.com: http://www.businessdictionary.com/definition/standard-operating-procedure-SOP.html.

- **Forms and Verbiage**

  Include examples of all of the forms your team might use, and include instructions about how to complete them correctly. In addition, prepare and compile verbiage (or guidelines) for patient interaction that you want your team to use consistently:

  - Answering the phone
  - Collection of new patient information
  - Greeting the patient
  - Conducting the patient interview
  - Handing-off to the next team member
  - Treatment planning
  - Overcoming objections and complaints
  - Scheduling
  - Asking for referrals

- **Patient Correspondence**

  Most of your patient correspondence these days will be electronic, either by email, text or by social media contact. Regardless of your medium, you'll want to automate as much as you can. Keep samples of each type of correspondence in your Operations Manual, along with an SOP about how to set them up and when to send them.

Your purpose for building an Operations Manual is to help you manage the systems you create, so you leave as little as possible to chance. Whenever a team member has a question or problem, or is asked to cover someone else's job or take on a new responsibility, the first place they should be able to find information is in your Operations Manual.

Building your Operations Manual from the ground up may take some time, but it doesn't have to be overwhelming. (Remember, one box at a time). You can ask key members of your team for help, and add to it as you find it necessary.

To make the task as simple as possible, take the time to plan the structure or outline of your Operations Manual first; so that as your practice grows, you add more services, staff, and functions, your Operations Manual will grow organically. Our team can also assist you in creating effective protocols and systems, as well as work with you and your team to implement them for sustainability. Contact DMI Coaching for assistance.

5. Set up sound planning and financial systems.

As the business owner or practice manager, you will most likely want to maintain responsibility for planning and managing the financial systems of your business, rather than delegating it to someone else.

First, you'll want to know the basics of budgeting, and set up systems to track revenue, expenses, and profit to measure your performance against your budget. Virtually any businessperson worth the title knows that. But let's take it a few steps further.

Do you know exactly how many patients/treatments/procedures it takes to meet your monthly, quarterly, and yearly budget? If your goal is to raise your income, do you know how many more patients/treatments/procedures it will take to do that?

Get out your calculator, use a computer spreadsheet, or grab a pencil and paper, and do the math yourself. Divide your current annual gross revenue by the number of patients you treat every year. That gives you a "revenue per patient" number. Now do the same with expenses. Divide your current annual gross expenses by the number of patients you treat every year. That yields your annual "cost per patient" of doing business.

Do you know your "break even" point? In other words, how much money do you need to collect so that your revenue meets your fixed expenses? (As a reminder, break-even is the step before you earn a profit.) How many patients does that figure represent?

Let's take the math a step deeper. If your analytics don't provide you the statistics, divide your annual revenue-per-patient and cost-per-patient by 12. That gives you monthly figures. Go one level further: divide those numbers by the total effective treatment hours in an average month. You can drill down and determine what it costs per hour to have a patient in the chair, and how much revenue that hour in the chair brings in.

Once you know your revenue and cost numbers, per patient, if you want to increase your profit you'll see several possibilities.

a. You could look at areas to reduce costs. Do you negotiate with your vendors? What is your procedure, your policy, for deciding on a supplier? Are you sure you're getting the best possible price? We recommend that you negotiate your fixed costs (rent, utilities, supplies, equipment) quarterly if you can, annually for sure.

b.You could raise your fees. After all, do you set your fees based on your revenue goals? Or do you set them based on your "gut feeling" for "what the market will bear?" Do you evaluate your fees compared to the fees in your area? We know of successful practices who decide on an acceptable profit margin first, setting aside that percentage of revenue first, and then running the business on the rest.

c. You could ask for, and reward, patient referrals. If you are not currently tracking where your new business comes from, that's an important system to design and implement.

d. You could improve your treatment plan acceptance rates, by designing, implementing, and perfecting a communication system that relies on building rapport, exploring and understanding your patient's deep needs, and learning to help patients overcome their resistance to treatment.

Each of those possibilities will require a system or perhaps several systems to track and measure your success.

6. Conduct regular "systems update" meetings with your team.

Meeting regularly once a week for half an hour ensures everything is running smoothly. Encourage your team to be "systems minded," such that when they become frustrated because something isn't working the way it should, they think first about the system, then about the person who might have been responsible. Remember, it may not be a personnel problem at all!

Review and discuss what's working, what's not working, and progress toward individual, departmental, and overall practice goals.

7. Monitor and track important systems where everyone can see them.

Important goals like controlling overhead, increasing revenue, or improving efficiency all require focus by the entire team. Wall charts, white dry-erase boards, progress posters and analytics are extremely valuable tools to keep your team motivated and focused on managing their systems. Post them in the break room or back office so team members (not necessarily patients) can see them.

Summary: use systems to create a "Team of CEOs."

Once you begin creating systems to handle the day-to-day routine of your business, you will find your team becoming far less frustrated, and more responsible for their own job performance. Once you manage your systems, you can lead your team to become a "Team of CEOs," each accountable one hundred percent for their own success. And leading a "team of CEOs" will transform your practice.

In the next Chapter, we'll show you how.

Ideas for Action

1. Set goals for all areas of your practice in terms of revenue, new business, cost reductions, etc.
2. Conduct a "systems audit" of your practice to determine if you have the systems in place to support those goals.

   - ✓ What systems do you have in place right now?
   - ✓ Does everyone on your team know about them?
   - ✓ Who is responsible for each system?
   - ✓ Is the system working?
   - ✓ Where do you need a system that you don't currently have?

   Based on your audit, identify areas that need systems

3. If you don't currently have an operations manual for your practice, begin building one.
   - ✓ Ask each team member to write down what they do each day/create a job description for their position
   - ✓ Ask each team member to design a checklist for each procedure they are responsible for
   - ✓ Create an outline/file structure for your operations manual. Include:
     - Verbiage (phone, hand-off, payment planning, etc.)
     - Form letters (appointment confirmation, reminders, thank you notes, requests for feedback)
     - Patient/Doctor/Administrative forms, by department or area of responsibility

- All systems: phone/utilities/purchasing/billing/communication/etc.

4. Contact our office to help you. **www.dmicoaching.com**

Chapter 11: Leading Your Team to Become a "Team of CEOs"

"You manage things, you lead people."

~ Rear Adm. Grace Hopper

How do you get people to be responsible, accountable for the work they do every day? How do you make sure they are doing things consistently, impeccably? How do you get them to "own" their job?

Do you manage them? Or do you lead them?

What's the difference between a manager and a leader?[17]

Managers	Leaders
Create goals	Create a vision
Maintain the status quo	Promote change
Control risks	Take risks
Think short-term	Think long-range
Rely on proven, existing skills	Learn new skills
Copy the behavior of others	Express their own uniqueness
Build systems and processes	Build relationships
Direct others	Coach others
Have employees	Create fans

In Chapter 10, we discussed the value of creating systems for your practice, so that people are absolutely clear about policies, procedures, and practices. Setting up systems is a function of **management**, which is vital to your practice.

Every successful business needs management. Setting the goals, controlling the risks, building the systems, and directing others to follow the rules are important to any business's survival.

---

[17] Arruda, William. (2016, 11/15). 9 Differences Between Being A Leader And A Manager. ***Forbes.*** Retrieved from: https://www.forbes.com/

But employees are not necessarily inspired by "managers." They do what's required, they expect rewards and consequences for their compliance. They're not particularly interested in innovation or change. They go along to get along. They collect a paycheck.

If you, as the business owner or practice manager, really want a high-performing team who are excited and enthusiastic about their work, who own the systems you create, and hold themselves accountable and responsible for the results of their work, you're going to want to develop your **leadership** skills.

Developing your own leadership skills will help you create a "team of CEOs."

Your Role as a Leader

> *The CEO helps a transformation succeed by communicating its significance, modeling the desired changes, building a strong top team, and getting personally involved.*[18]

As a leader, **you are responsible for communicating your long-term vision for your practice**, and personally engaging your team to help you achieve that vision.

[18] Aiken, C. and Keller, S. (2007, February). The CEO's role in leading transformation. *McKinsey & Company Organization*. Retrieved from: http://www.mckinsey.com/business-functions/organization

Openly communicate what it means for them to be with you on your journey. Be willing to make your desire for change personal to them, to communicate about it openly, and to celebrate every time the team succeeds.

That means you have to **walk your talk**. *"You must be the change you want to see in the world,"* said Gandhi. Show your team with your own behavior and willingness to communicate openly that you are committed to transforming your practice.

Building a team of committed players requires you to **be ruthless about determining who has the required skill, ability, and motivation to play the game with you**. That means you've got to hold people accountable, and teach them to hold each other accountable, for their results.

As a leader, you must **be willing to do the work**, to roll up your sleeves and get personally involved in helping your team solve problems, particularly those problems that have risky consequences. If that means you have to sit down at the computer to work through a problem with your accounts receivables, or sit at the front desk to observe and participate during a high-call volume morning, or learn to fix your equipment yourself to understand its complexity. Teams are inspired by leaders who truly understand the components of the game.

Lead Your Team to Hold Themselves Accountable

It's 12:00pm on Friday, time for your monthly team meeting. Everyone is there but your hygienist. When she arrives at 12:15, your office manager takes charge, "We all agreed to be here at 12:00pm. What happened?" The hygienist turns red in the face, stammers an explanation, and the meeting moves on. Later in the meeting, your treatment coordinator reports her case acceptance rate for the week, and it's below goal. Your front office, treatment coordinator, hygienist, and office manager all pepper each other with tough questions about their methods, and offer honest, direct suggestions about how to improve acceptance.

What's going on here? Team accountability, that's what. Sounds shocking, doesn't it?

According to the *Harvard Business Review*: in the weakest teams, there is no accountability; in mediocre teams, bosses are the source of accountability; and **in high performance teams, peers manage the vast majority of performance problems with one another**.[19]

In other words, in a high-performing team, members hold themselves and one another accountable.

So how do you make that happen?

[19] Grenny, J. (2014, 05/30). The Best Teams Hold Themselves Accountable. ***Harvard Business Review***. Retrieved from: https://hbr.org/2014/05/the-best-teams-hold-themselves-accountable.

Making that shift requires immense amounts of trust. And **trust is the result of consistent, repeated behavior over time.**

And if you've never had the privilege of leading a self-managing team, it's going to **require a massive commitment** from you and everyone on the team to **keep their agreements**, **manage their area of responsibility with integrity**, and **communicate truthfully** about their results.

To **lead** your team to high performance, focus on these elements:

1. **Set Expectations**

   Let new team members know the team expects them to hold themselves and others, including you, accountable for their results and behavior.

2. **Lead By Example**

   Show them, with your own behavior, that you are committed to holding yourself accountable. If you're late, own it. If you don't meet your own goals, case acceptance or behavior, own it. Don't let team members hear you grousing about someone behind their back! Model the behavior you want to see in them.

   Invest some time each day, either formally or informally, in teaching effective communication and accountability skills. Practice with your team, using recent, real-life examples from their own jobs, to help them learn and remember the new skills.

3. Catch Team Members "doing it right"

When you see a team member effectively owning a problem, admitting a mistake, or effectively holding another team member to account, acknowledge it. Heap praise on that team member. Use this team member as an example in your morning huddle and staff meeting. Reward the behavior you want to see.

4. Establish and Manage Your Systems.

Go back and re-read Chapter 10! Make sure that you have established clear, documented systems, for every aspect of your practice. Train your staff to manage their performance with job descriptions, checklists and worksheets that everyone agrees to follow.

5. Help Team Members Set Their Own Performance Goals, and Offer Meaningful Rewards for Reaching orExceeding Them.

It may sound revolutionary, but some of the most successful dental practices in business tie their team's salaries to their job "metrics" or Key Performance Indicators (KPIs) for each area of responsibility. For example, consider employee or team bonuses or commissions for new patient referrals, ideas that promote cost savings or improved efficiency, improved patient satisfaction survey results, and so forth. Be creative. Ask your team for ideas about rewards that might be meaningful to them and productive for your practice.

6. **Celebrate Team Victories.**

   Whenever your team reaches a goal, celebrate! Throw a party. Host a picnic. Take everyone to a ball game. Send out an email/text blast to your team, acknowledging your team's success and thanking them for their help in making it happen. After all, behavior that gets rewarded gets repeated.

Manage your Systems, Lead your People

Much of the source of frustration, disappointment, or drama among team members can be traced to miscommunication, misunderstandings, and broken agreements (not keeping one's word).

When you've created the systems that define their roles, responsibilities, and procedures, there is little room for team members to "wing it "or just go through the motions. When you provide the systems that help your team members know what to do, how to do it, and who is ultimately accountable for their results, you give them permission to manage their own word and acknowledge those teammates who break their agreements. You create a culture that is much calmer, more rewarding, and personally fulfilling for everyone.

And when your team is trained and rewarded for managing systems, it frees you up to do what you love best and lead your team to success.

Ideas for Action: Create a High-Performing Team

1. Establish a "Leadership Initiative" in your practice. Commit to yourself that you will do whatever it takes to create a high-performance team. Give yourself a deadline.

2. Take inventory of your own motivation for leadership. Ask yourself what "fires you up" about your practice. What is rewarding to you? What do you love most about your practice, your patients, and your team? If you could change one thing about the way your practice works, what would it be?

3. Interview every member of your team. Find out why they chose to work in the dental field. Find out what they love about their job. Ask them what they would change about their job if they could, and why they would change it. Ask "How am I doing as a leader in our practice? What could I be doing differently? Are there any promises I have not followed through on?" The answers might surprise you!

4. Contact us at **www.dmicoaching.com** to help you create the high-performing team and move your practice to a higher level of satisfaction and financial success.

Conclusion

Imagine a practice...

- ✓ that is growing, vital, innovative, and seems to "manage itself"
- ✓ that experiences dramatic growth, as your existing patients start referring a steady stream of their friends, family, and colleagues
- ✓ that achieves 5-Star Reviews from patients thrilled by the outstanding service you and your team deliver
- ✓ with treatment acceptance rates of 50...60...70% and the dramatic increase in your income that represents these results

Imagine a Workplace...

- ✓ that is bustling, and personally fulfilling, where everyone knows how to build rapport, communicate honestly and openly, and work within systems to hold each other accountable
- ✓ with a thriving culture, staffed by a team of individuals who can proudly say "I am changing the world one patient at a time"
- ✓ with an excited, inspired and determined team, committed to achieving and exceeding your practice's goals

Imagine a Team...

- ✓ full of happy, productive individuals who are dedicated to getting to know your patients as people and providing them outstanding care and stellar customer service
- ✓ committed to smooth treatment planning, hand-offs, scheduling, and follow-up systems that run like clockwork
- ✓ who experience "wins" with every patient your practice serves

Just Imagine...

- ✓ finally being able to take those vacations, buy the sporty new car and purchase the beautiful home you always dreamed of
- ✓ transforming yourself, your team, your patients, your business and your life

These results, and so many more, can arise from your passion for doing what you love and loving what you do, your determination to overcome obstacles and move forward, and your willingness to get support when you need it.

It's a great time to be a dentist. Rapid advances in technology give you the opportunity to heal so many people and add richness to their lives. You ease their pain and create the beautiful smiles that give your patients confidence. They can now apply for jobs they never dreamed they could get, finally ask that special someone out on a date, or speak in public for the first time without embarrassment. You make a difference in your patients' lives.

Isn't that why you became a dentist in the first place?

And...

Dentistry requires more than just clinical excellence. It requires you to be a CEO, creating an economy for yourself and your team. It requires you to inspire others to achieve peak performance. It requires you to master effective communication skills and model those skills to your team. It requires you to be an HR director, accountant, marketing guru, systems manager, a continuous student of new technologies, and so much more.

Also, most importantly, remember the old adage “People buy the salesman first and their product second”. What are you doing right now to improve you and your team’s circle of influence? Influence is not about the expertise you gained in dental school. Influence is about your patients feeling heard, valued and understood so they are motivated to take action *Now* on your advice and direction.

Without assistance, proper guidance, and effective coaching, you’d need a superhero’s cape to perform all of these roles effectively.

That’s where we come in.

We wrote this book to inspire you to **create the practice you desire, achieve the massive growth you know you can achieve**, and ultimately, **transform your life** and **experience the joy, prosperity, and fulfillment you deserve.**

And we also know that gathering more information or knowledge does not necessarily lead to success. The key to success, whether you're a dentist, business owner, or CEO, is knowing how and when to implement and **take action on that knowledge.**

How Greater Success Happens

"Let Today Be The Day You Give Up Who You've Been, For Who You Can Become"
-Hal Elrod

Any leader, athlete, or performer recognizes the value of working with a gifted coach who can help them push past their limiting beliefs and break through to the next level. A great coach will help you see what you cannot see yourself, help you move past the blind spots, and serve your patients, engage your team.

For over 20 years, we have worked with dentists just like you, coaching and mentoring to do the dentistry you love while achieving the ultimate success easily and effortlessly.

Isn't it time to take your practice to the next level?

Don't you think you deserve it?

As Dr. Jeannie Ju said in the forward "*I would not be where I am now if it were not for Patrice and Shelly*".

Go to this link Now to schedule your complimentary consultation so you can achieve your goals.
http://www.dmicoaching.com

Printed in Dunstable, United Kingdom

91223992R00103